How to Buy and Manage a

FRANCHISE

Joseph Mancuso and Donald Boroian

A Fireside Book
Published by Simon & Schuster

New York   London   Toronto   Sydney   Tokyo   Singapore

FIRESIDE
Rockefeller Center
1230 Avenue of the Americas
New York, New York 10020

Designed by Richard Oriolo
Manufactured in the United States of America

10 9 8 7 6 5 4 3 2 1

Library of Congress Cataloging-in-Publication Data

Mancuso, Joseph.
    How to buy and manage a franchise / Joseph
Mancuso and   Donald Boroian.
       p. cm.
    "A Fireside book."
    Includes bibliographical references and index.
    1. Franchises (Retail trade) 2. Business
enterprises—Purchasing.
  I. Boroian, Donald D. II. Title
HF5429.23.M36 1993
658.8'708—dc20   93-14133
                             CIP

ISBN: 0-671-76775-5

Acknowledgments

The authors would like to acknowledge several special contributors without whom the writing of this book would not have been possible. All of these persons have both enriched our lives with their friendship and contributed greatly to our knowledge of franchising: Arthur Lipper, former Publisher, *Venture* magazine; Jules W. Lederer, former Chairman, Budget Rent A Car; Andrew Kostecka, former Franchise Specialist with the U.S. Department of Commerce; and Kegham and Charles Giragosian, formerly Presidents and Chairmen of Chicken Unlimited.

We would like to thank the following members of the staff of Mr. Boroian's franchise consulting firm, Francorp, Inc.: Michael H. Baum, Executive Vice President; Mark C. Siebert, Senior Vice President; Richard Gosswiller, Senior Vice President; and Joseph Busch, Vice President. Special thanks also go to Patrick Boroian, former president of Francorp and now with Sprout Group, and to all the franchisors and franchisees whose stories appear in Chapter 6.

Contents

Contents

Chapter One

The American Dream with a Safety Net: An Introduction to Franchising

Fred DeLuca needed cash. At seventeen, he was ready for college, but unless he raised some money fast, he knew he couldn't cover his first-year expenses at Connecticut's University of Bridgeport. As it would turn out, DeLuca's solution for financing his college education would lead to one of the biggest franchising success stories of the late eighties and early nineties. But back in 1965, all he wanted was a financial fix.

DeLuca approached a wealthy family friend for the money. He recalls hoping that Peter Buck, a nuclear physicist, would "reach into his pocket and pull out a big stack of hundred-dollar bills." Instead, Buck offered something more valuable—a business proposition. Instead of a gift or loan, he would give the youngster $1,000 to open a submarine sandwich shop. And so Pete's Submarines of Bridgeport was born.

After a slow start (and a name change), the partners added fifteen more sandwich shops in the following eight years. The chain had potential for further growth, but the traditional method of building and operating company-owned stores was proving to be slow and costly. The choice of an alternative wasn't hard to make. McDonald's and Kentucky Fried Chicken, among others, had set an excellent example by franchising, and it was in that direction that DeLuca turned to expand his business.

More than twenty-five years after it was started as a collegiate money-making venture, this submarine sandwich idea has truly paid off. DeLuca and Buck's business has become the pacesetter among sandwich chains, setting a growth standard believed to be untouched by even megaoutlet food giants such as McDonald's or Domino's Pizza. In a single year—1988—Subway, as the franchise is now called, opened more than one thousand outlets, a feat never previously accomplished by a single chain.

Of course, opening a sandwich shop isn't a rocket-scientist type of proposition. All one needs is money (which, as has been demonstrated, can be *someone else's*) and desire. Even making that shop a success isn't a superhuman task. Combine hard work, a good product, and a reasonably decent location, and you can be the local roast beef and salami king. But to establish and successfully duplicate such a store a few thousand times across the country and around the world takes more than a profitable outlet (or even a few such outlets). It takes one of two things: (1) Nearly unlimited capital (quite literally in the billions of dollars) to finance such growth; or (2) the proven, synergistic power of franchising.

So if you happen to have a couple of billion dollars lying around in a family trust, or a friendly banker whose loan checks come preprinted with nine zeros, then what follows will likely not be of much interest to you. But if you have a desire to become part of—or simply learn more about—franchising, the successful and growing form of business the U.S. Department of Commerce has called "the wave of the future," this book is the source you've been looking for.

Why This Book?

As franchising has grown in prominence and performance, it has attracted wide coverage in the media—some positive, some negative; some aimed at potential franchisees, some at franchisors; some purely analytical, some philosophical and esoteric. But what was missing was a comprehensive, easy to read (and perhaps *fun* to read) book that tied it all together—a book that combined practical and useful information for both franchisees and franchisors with unbiased reporting and interpretation of the development and influence of franchising. The challenge, then, is to fill this information gap.

This book sets out to be the *only* book anyone (be they franchisees, franchisors, or even just curious consumers) needs to read about franchising. And that's not just a boast or some lofty goal—it is our *personal* mission as authors.

Who Should Read This Book?

Perhaps it sounds too simple: anyone with any interest in franchising. But it's true. This book was written with the widest possible variety of readers in mind. Whether you are interested in purchasing a franchise (that is, becoming a *franchisee*), developing an existing business into a franchise (becoming a *franchisor*), or simply learning more about the form of business responsible for more than one-third of all retail sales in the United States, this book will inform, educate, and perhaps even amaze you.

Do you dream of becoming your own boss but are wary of striking out on your own? We'll help you assess whether you're ready (financially *and* emotionally) to become a franchisee. Are you ready to buy a franchise, but not sure which one to choose?

We'll give you some valuable advice to help narrow which franchises are best suited to you.

Perhaps you own a small (or even not so small) business and are considering expansion. We'll help you answer two questions of paramount importance when it comes to considering a franchise program: (1) Is your business franchisable? and, (2) if so, what is the best way to go about it? The fact is times have never been better to consider expansion through franchising, for anyone who owns or operates a successful business. There is definitely an audience of qualified potential franchisees available. Big corporations, including many Fortune 500 companies, are stripping away layers of middle managers with layoffs and early retirements. Add to this pool of talent the growing number of executives whose jobs have been "leveraged" out of existence (due to buy outs, mergers, and other corporate reshufflings), and you have an experienced and professional class of people ready for a new challenge. For many of these people—and others ready for a change—franchising is the best choice.

Joe's brother, John Mancuso, is a good example of a new breed of franchisee. He owned and operated a small machine shop in Hartford, Connecticut, for the past half dozen years. He also was a customer of the local Physicians Weight Loss Center in Hartford, and trimmed down from a hefty 270 pounds to close to 210 pounds. He was thrilled with his weight loss—so much so that he sold his machine shop and used the proceeds to acquire the franchise location where he had lost weight. Rather than start a new business in an area that interested him (but in which he had no practical experience), he bought the franchise and the national reputation and source of knowledge that went with it—a franchise that he knew was effective, because it helped *him* lose weight.

John had never anticipated being involved with franchising, but at the age of forty, he too came to marvel at the power of the concept. (But, as you'll learn later in this book, John lost more than just weight. That was another motivation to write this book.)

What Is Franchising?

Franchising is a broad term that describes a relationship between two or more parties. In general, the purpose of this relationship is to distribute goods and/or services. The two primary types of franchise systems in the United States are *product* or *tradename* franchising and *business-format* franchising. Product or tradename franchising is franchising in its most limited form: A manufacturer grants another party a license to sell goods produced by the manufacturer. Principal examples of this form of franchising include sales of cars through dealerships, gasoline through service stations, and soft drinks through local bottlers.

For the purposes of this book, we will almost always be discussing the other type—business-format franchising. We will refer to it by the simpler term *franchising.* Under business-format franchising, a business owner or manager (the franchisor) allows someone to market products or services using her name, trademark, and, most importantly, her prescribed business format— thus the name *business-format franchising.* (Frequently—in fact,

The Franchise Line:
THOROUGHBREDS

Proven winners for the long stretch
McDonald's (*hamburgers*)
Holiday Inn (*hotels*)
Budget Rent A Car (*car rentals*)
Midas (*mufflers and car service*)
Blockbuster Video (*video rental*)
Merle Harmon's Fan Fair (*imprinted sportswear*)
Domino's (*pizza delivery*)
Culligan (*water treatment*)
Dairy Queen (*soft-serve ice cream*)
am/pm mini market (*convenience stores*)

usually—the products sold are *not* provided by the franchisor.) In return for use of the name and system, *the franchisee*—as that person or organization is called—pays a fee and, usually, an ongoing royalty (in the form of a percentage of sales). Moreover, the franchisee pays all the costs of going into business. The effect of business-format franchising is to make it less a system of distribution than a system of proliferation or expansion.

There is a bit of irony about the division between the two types: While business-format franchising is what the general public thinks of as franchising, it is product or tradename franchising that is responsible for nearly 80 percent of all franchising revenues—even though its numbers of outlets and employees have steadily declined over the last two decades. One major reason for this disparity in revenue is product and tradename franchising includes automotive dealership sales, and, as you may have figured out, it takes quite a few Big Macs to match the price tag of a single Cadillac!

Examples of the Three Types of Franchises

Business-Format Franchises
1. McDonald's
2. AAMCO Transmission
3. Molly Maid

Product or Tradename Franchising
1. Ford dealerships
2. Shell stations
3. Coca-Cola bottlers

Conversion Franchises
1. Century 21
2. Comprehensive Accounting Services
3. Econo Lodges of America

An additional type of franchising is called *conversion franchising*. This is an adaptation of business-format franchising designed to bring formerly independent businesspeople the collective power of a national name and national advertising. A well-known and very successful example of a conversion franchise is Century 21, an affiliation of previously established real estate agents who have become the leader in their industry through the collective power of franchising.

The Advantages of Franchising

Franchising has grown and continues to grow because it provides distinct advantages compared to traditional means of business ownership/expansion.

For the franchisor, franchising is a means of expansion which does not require huge infusions of capital. It also can provide an effective mechanism for achieving deep market penetration ahead of the competition. Franchising is a viable alternative to the costly and time-consuming practice of opening

---

The Franchise Line:
DARK HORSES

Lesser known but up and coming

Jersey Mike's Subs (*sub sandwiches*)
USA Baby (*baby furniture and accessories*)
TRC Temporary Services (*temporary help*)
Rocky Mountain Chocolate (*retail candy*)
Nix Check Cashing (*storefront financial services*)
Filterfresh (*brew-by-the-cup coffee service*)
We Care Hair (*budget hair salons*)
Academy of Learning (*computer software training*)
Gloria Jean's Coffee Bean (*retail gourmet coffee*)

---

additional company-owned (which means company-financed and -managed) stores. With franchisees to help raise capital, share risks, and provide steady and dedicated management, corporate growth and expansion can be swift and relatively painless.

For the franchisee, it is a shot at realizing the American dream of owning a business, but with much of the risk removed. In effect, the franchisee is able to launch a new business without many of the attendant growing pains. Someone else has already made—and learned from—the most important and obvious mistakes, ironed out the wrinkles, and refined a system that works efficiently. It is like a cook using a recipe created and tested by a master chef—he or she can be pretty confident of getting good results on the first attempt.

Franchising also provides franchisees with the additional comfort of ongoing support. While they are in business for themselves, they are never in business *by* themselves. It means being able to benefit from the use of a prominent name and the collective strength of a large chain when purchasing supplies and advertising.

From the standpoint of consumers, franchising delivers familiarity and consistency. Consumers expect the pizza they buy in Boston will be identical to the one they purchased from the same franchise in San Francisco. Ditto for hamburgers, haircuts, and hotel rooms. Not only are consumers reassured by this dependability, but they have come to demand it, and all other factors being equal, will reward it with their patronage.

Three Reasons Franchising Succeeds

Of course, it would be overly simplistic to claim franchising has become successful because it's a *good* form of business. Three specific reasons franchising has succeeded (and continues to do so) are that it *is good* for the three separate groups who have connections to it: consumers, business owners, and franchisees.

Franchising Is Good for Consumers

For reasons of consistency, quality, and (in most cases) price, the franchising of goods and services has been a boon to consumers. While many have disparaged franchising as being responsible for the so-called "blanding of America," a closer analysis of the evidence indicates that franchising has *broadened* consumers' choices. For example, thirty or forty years ago, consumers outside of California and Texas were generally not exposed to Mexican cuisine. The same goes for pizza outside of big cities in the Northeast. Today, thanks primarily to franchise chains such as Taco Bell, Pizza Hut, and others, these once exotic foods have proliferated from coast to coast and are among America's favorite foods. Even the Russians now have the Golden Arches in Moscow—and from the early reports, they seem to treat the hamburger as a gourmet meal.

Franchising Is Good for Business Owners

If Subway's Fred DeLuca had a hard time coming up with hundreds of dollars when he founded his business twenty-five or so years ago, imagine the difficulty he would have faced raising that mythical $1 billion we mentioned earlier. But without the power of franchising, Subway would have needed *at least* $1 billion to reach the preeminence it has achieved in the same timeframe. Franchising gives a new business the tools and ability to take on an established independent in the same market. For example, the White Castle hamburger chain, one of the pioneers of fast food, has expanded slowly, plowing the profits of existing stores into new company-owned units. After some seventy years, its chain boasts more than three hundred company-owned outlets. Fairly successful, right? Unless, of course, you measure White Castle's accomplishments against an "upstart" chain that chose franchising as its vehicle of expansion. In less than half that time, McDonald's opened more than thirteen thousand stores. That's more than *forty times* as many outlets as White Castle! And McDonald's continues to widen the

The Franchise Line:
$2 BETS

Low-cost franchises

Signs Now! (*fast signs*)

Subway (*sub sandwiches*)

Coverall (*janitorial service*)

H & R Block (*tax preparation*)

Proforma (*business forms and supplies*)

Priority Management Systems (*management training*)

Decorating Den (*mobile interior decorating*)

Novus Windshield Repair (*chip and crack repair*)

White Hen Pantry (*convenience store*)

Stained Glass Overlay (*stained-glass effects on existing windows*)

gap, opening new outlets at a clip of approximately one every twelve hours. Now they are starting to proliferate in the countries that were once behind the Iron Curtain—we bet they'll be the first to the moon, too!

Franchising Is Good for People Who Want to Become Franchisees

How many businesses could a novice enter with an investment of less than $75,000 (often, less than $50,000) and, after a training period of a week or two, begin operations, secure that there is a 95 percent chance of that business still existing in a year? Yet those are very real possibilities for a new franchisee. Add to that the ability to operate a new business with the strength of a nationwide (or regionwide) name and reputation, and it is clear that franchising truly provides a unique opportunity for business success. In essence, franchisees benefit from all the advantages of both independent and company-owned businesses, without most of the inherent disadvantages. Think about this: If you were an entrepreneur in Poland, Hungary, or eastern Germany—or even, as the free-market explosion continues, in Russia or Ukraine—how would you like to have your region's first franchise for McDonald's, Kentucky Fried Chicken, Holiday Inns, or so on? The thought is so exciting it almost makes you want to pack it all up and relocate to eastern Europe!

Franchising by the Numbers

As is true of any form of business—or, indeed, with any individual business—a wealth of information about franchising can be garnered by studying its "bottom line." Since its growth and rise to prominence and all-pervasiveness, franchising has generated some truly impressive statistics:

- 35 cents of every retail dollar in the United States are spent at a franchised business.
- By the year 2000, that total should increase to 55 cents.
- In the decade of the 1980s, franchising's annual sales figures more than doubled, from $336 billion to an estimated $716 billion.
- By the year 2000, franchised sales are estimated to nearly double again and surpass $1 trillion per year.
- There are more than 542,000 franchise outlets in the United States, employing more than 7 million workers.
- It is estimated that a new franchised store opens in the United States every sixteen minutes.
- According to the U.S. Department of Commerce, franchised outlets have a failure rate of less than 5 percent per year, while Dun and Bradstreet claims more than 50 percent of new businesses fail during their first five years.

The Impact of Franchising

There is no doubt that franchising is a staggeringly successful form of doing business. Because franchising has become an integral part of the American way of life, it has had ramifications that affect areas far beyond the scope of business expansion. Franchising influences America and its tastes and preferences in myriad ways.

How all-pervasive is franchising? For an idea of its universality and popularity, you need look no further than its leading proponent, McDonald's. McDonald's claims:

- In any given year, 96 percent of all Americans walk through its doors.
- Every month, 59 percent of the population visits a McDonald's.
- Its daily traffic is more than 15 million customers.
- And, perhaps most interesting, it has given one out of every fifteen Americans their first job!

The Franchise Line: QUARTERHORSES

Moving fast

Discovery Zone (*childhood indoor recreation*)
The Body Shop (*environmentally friendly cosmetics*)
Krystal (*drive-through hamburgers*)
Mail Boxes Etc. (*mailboxes, office supplies, shipping services*)
Re/Max (*real estate brokerage*)
Port of Subs (*sub sandwiches*)
Jacki's (*aerobic exercise*)
Fast Frame (*picture framing*)
Auntie Anne's (*pretzels*)
Floor Coverings Int'l (*retail floor covering*)

Of course, McDonald's is far and away the leader not only in its market, but in all of franchising. However, even if those numbers merely represent franchising at its most successful, it's not difficult to do a little imaginative extrapolation. It would not be farfetched to claim that franchising touches the life of nearly every American *every day of every year.*

While you undoubtedly get fed up with McDonald's food intermittently and may occasionally swear to never eat there again, the odds are overwhelming that you *will* be back—because it's so dependable, convenient, and usually such a good deal.

Examining the Anti-Franchising Myths

Some detractors claim that because franchising relies on consistency and reliability, it promotes mediocrity and stifles individuality. But, upon closer scrutiny, this analysis doesn't hold up. On one hand, franchising does result in a certain amount of uniformity—*proven* uniformity, it should be noted. These systems are uniform because *they work.* However, at a deeper level, franchising has been a great force for individuality. By giving more people the opportunity to successfully own businesses than ever before, franchising has provided an important and viable alternative to climbing the corporate ladder or toiling in an unfulfilling dead-end job.

At the same time, franchising has enabled the entrepreneurial owners of relatively small and/or new businesses to effectively compete against larger corporations or long-entrenched local competition. Franchising makes rapid growth possible without huge amounts of capital, which means that a well-run business with a point of difference has a better chance of expanding than ever before.

There is also no reason to assume because a product or service is consistent and reliable, it is necessarily mediocre. In fact, if that were the case, its long-term chances for success would be *reduced,* since consumers today more than ever look

The Franchise Line:
COMING FROM BEHIND

Franchise turnarounds
  Burger King (*hamburgers*)
  PIP Printing (*fast printing*)
  International House of Pancakes (*family restaurant*)
  Ben Franklin (*craft stores*)
  Taco Bell (*Mexican food*)
  7-Eleven (*convenience store*)
  Computerland (*retail computers*)
  Popeyes Fried Chicken & Biscuits (*chicken and seafood*)

for the best value for their dollar. Nor does franchising stifle creativity. Instead, franchising encourages entrepreneurs to turn their ideas into reality and to allow others to share in their success.

This ties in with another myth about franchising—that it puts small businesses, the so-called "mom and pop" operations, out of business. In some cases, franchised businesses *have* replaced neighborhood businesses—grocery stores, for example. But the "mom and pop" proprietors of corner grocery stores have been replaced by the same kinds of people (many times, the same *exact* people) who now own 7-Elevens or Convenient Food Marts. And, neighborhood purists aside, the truth is these franchised outlets are more profitable, better organized, and more easily resold than the family corner grocery.

Franchising is also an excellent vehicle for introducing new (or unfamiliar) and specialized businesses. Examples of these include ethnic foods (the aforementioned Mexican food and pizza restaurants), single-focus car-care services (such as mufflers, oil changes, or transmissions), and business-oriented services (such as typing/word processing, accounting, and even a variety of consulting services).

Good . . . But Not Perfect

As good as franchising is, it's not for everyone *or* for every business. For example, a person who can't take direction well would probably not fare well as a franchisee. A person who has to be in control of every facet of his or her business wouldn't survive long as a franchisor, where you have to delegate to and cooperate with franchisees.

As for individual businesses, if they are locally oriented, or dependent upon a particular site or personality, they too may fail in the world of franchising. And, of course, there are other factors to consider.

In general, businesses with small profit margins, low sales figures, or high prices (but small volume) do *not* make good candidates for franchising. (We'll examine—in depth—the traits that *do* make a good franchise in Chapter 7.)

Keep These Thoughts in Mind

As you'd expect of any new venture—especially a new business venture—franchising needs a considerable amount of soul searching and self-realization. As either a franchisee or franchisor, you should have clearly defined expectations of what you will put in and get out of your business. Although we will thoroughly examine the general needs and desires of both of these groups in later chapters, following are four general thoughts that you should be aware of as you consider franchising:

Don't Expect to Get Rich Quick

Any business, even with a tried and tested operating system, is a gamble. While franchising is a more successful system of business expansion, there are no sure things—not for franchisees or franchisors. You should be in either program for the long haul, not for a quick fix. The rewards will presumably come, but they take work.

Are You Determined to Succeed?

There are plenty of places in this world for nine-to-fivers, but (with very few exceptions) running a franchised outlet or a franchise company is *not* among them. As a franchisee (especially early on), you are apt to run your outlet from open to close. As a franchisor, you will need to work long and hard to both establish your company and nurture it along to success. These are heady challenges, requiring stamina and determination. Are you up to it? Remember, entrepreneurship, like Thomas Edison's definition of *genius,* is often 1 percent inspiration and 99 percent perspiration.

Does Franchising Fit Your Personality?

Do you chafe at rules and regulations imposed by others? Since following a franchise program is basically following the dictates of someone else, strongly independent people may not make good franchisees. As a franchisor, you need to teach, support, and

---

The Franchise Line:
SADDLE HORSES

Own them for the pleasure as much as the money
Little Professor Book Stores (*books*)
Travel Travel (*travel agency*)
Jazzercize (*aerobic exercise*)
Petland (*pet store*)
Conroy's Flowers (*florist*)
Tinderbox (*gifts*)
Supercuts (*bargain haircutting*)
Baskin-Robbins (*ice cream*)
Johnny Rockets (*'50s-style diner restaurant*)
American Sock Shop (*retail hosiery*)

---

inspire your franchisees; if you are not a good "people person," you are probably not going to make a good franchisor.

Be Realistic about Your Goals and the Time Needed to Achieve Them

As a franchisee, are you planning to break your franchise's sales record in your first week of operation? As a franchisor, do you picture your chain being mentioned in the same breath as McDonald's after its first year? There is nothing wrong with ambition and goals, but your goals need to be realistic and achievable, lest you feel (quite unnecessarily) you are failing. For example, a person best learns to swim when he is put in a pool of water about chest-high, so he can approach swimming at his own pace. When a person is put in a pool which is over his head, there is a great deal of noise and kicking and thrashing—this is panicking (or, at worst, drowning), not swimming.

Other important factors to consider (we will cover these in later chapters) are your financial status, the cooperation and support of your family, your management skills, and your overall

---

The Franchise Line: OUT OF THE CORRAL

Franchises you can run from home

Advantage Refreshments (*vending*)
ServiceMaster (*carpet cleaning*)
Money Mailer (*cooperative couponing*)
Lawn Doctor (*lawn service*)
Sport-It (*sports equipment and apparel*)
Ident-A-Kid (*child identification*)
Servpro (*cleaning and restoration service*)
HouseMaster of America (*home warranties*)
Merry Maids (*maid service*)
Respond First Aid Systems (*first aid kit sales and service*)

temperament. The more you know about yourself and your desires, the better your chances of fulfilling those desires. We've designed special tests, which appear later in this book, to evaluate your suitability as a franchisee or the franchisability of your business (see Chapters 3 and 7).

Making the American Dream Come True

Franchising has become one of the most publicized and recognized forms of business extant. It can make the American dream of owning one's own business happen, with the "safety net" of being part of a larger entity. Franchising is a multibillion-dollar industry with roots on nearly every big city streetcorner or small-town Main Street. You have likely been patronizing franchises for years without giving it much thought. Franchising is a part of the fabric of American life.

But how did franchising reach this point? If you are considering becoming a franchisee or franchisor, you should be aware of the origins and development of this fascinating and successful form of business. In the next chapter, we will cover some of the important history in the field of franchising,

The Franchise Line:
JOE'S GLUE FACTORY

Need we say more?

TCBY (*yogurt*)
EconoLodge (*economy motel*)
Convenient Food Mart (*convenience store*)
Moto Photo (*fast photo finishing*)
Comprehensive Accounting (*accounting*)
Jiffy Lube (*fast lubrication*)
Ziebart (*rustproofing*)
General Business Service (*small business consulting*)

examining the successes—and the failures—that have contributed to its phenomenal growth.

And a very interesting history it is. For example, other than their huge impact on American life since the 1950s, what did Ray Kroc and Walt Disney have in common?

A hint: the answer has nothing to do with food or entertainment . . .

The History of Franchising

Franchising is a highly efficient, proven way to run an individual business and to expand a parent business. It provides built-in advantages (and can smooth out many disadvantages) in businesses that use it.

However, franchising is not a silver bullet, a magic wand, or an alchemist's trick. Neither is it foolproof. It has had its failures, some of them spectacular. But its overall track record is still one of its allures for both franchisees and franchisors.

Over the last half-century, franchising has flourished—not particularly at the expense of other forms of business, but on its own merits, carving out its unique and substantial niche. Because it works, it is prevalent; and because it is prevalent, it works.

Of course, it wasn't always that way.

Singer "Sews" the Seeds

While it may seem as if franchising skipped the infant stage and was born as a fully grown adult about thirty years ago, its roots stretch much farther back. Many casual observers are surprised to learn franchising did not begin with the construction of the first set of golden arches! What Ray Kroc did with McDonald's was to revolutionize a system that had existed in varying forms for decades. In fact, early uses of franchising can be traced back more than *one hundred years* before the first McDonald's burger was served up!

The Singer Sewing Machine Company is generally acknowledged as developing the first retail use of franchising as a way to sell and service its products. In the 1850s, Singer established a network of salesmen/dealers who paid Singer for the right to distribute sewing machines in a particular region. Although these arrangements were not completely successful for Singer and were discontinued after about ten years, Singer had planted the seeds for franchising's future use and eventual universal acceptance.

Enter Product or Tradename Franchising

In the late nineteenth century, railroad and utility companies sought to speed their growth and spread their influence. The method they used was an embryonic form of franchising. By selling subsidiary rights to their names and/or systems to businesspeople or investor groups (who would foot the bill for construction), these entities could in effect more quickly open a new section of track or a new electric plant in the next town.

This led directly to the creation of what we now refer to as product or tradename franchising. As we explained in the last chapter, product or tradename franchising is a distribution system based on the granting of a license. It allows the franchisee (or licensee) to sell goods produced by the franchisor or to produce finished goods from proprietary materials or formulas supplied by the franchisor. This form of franchising has had its biggest impact in the areas of automobile sales, gasoline sales, and soft-drink bottling.

Developing Automobile Dealerships

The late 1890s and early 1900s saw the popular development of the automobile. In those early days, when there were literally hundreds of automobile manufacturers, the key to success was distribution of this new product. General Motors, founded in 1908, set up one of the first successful automobile dealership systems by licensing independent salesmen to sell its cars. The dealer purchased the land and built the buildings for the dealership, then bought cars at a discount from the manufacturer. This method not only enabled the automaker to distribute its cars effectively but also could help GM build brand loyalty and provide dedicated outlets for customer service through aggressive dealerships.

By 1920s and 1930s, the basic franchise relationship between the automobile industry and the dealers was well established. Dealerships (or, in effect, franchises) were granted to individuals who agreed to keep at least a minimum basic inventory of the manufacturers' cars and spare parts on hand. This practice has continued (with modifications and adaptations) to the present day, the biggest change being the number of different manufacturers represented on a single automobile lot.

The latest chapter in the relationship between automobile manufacturers and franchising involves the many *new* brands of cars (some new only to the U.S. market) that have been appearing the last few years. Lexus, Infiniti, Acura, and Saturn are among the newcomers who are being aggressively and quickly rolled out through franchising. In many of these recent cases, the franchise agreements being used are much more detailed than the old dealer franchises. These agreements prescribe very definite systems to be used for the marketing and sales of these automobiles.

Fueling the Petroleum Industry's Success

While automobile manufacturers began franchising by design, oil companies were virtually forced into it by necessity. Early this century, oil companies operated most of their own gas stations, in direct competition with independent operators. It soon became evident the independents had a definite advantage over the oil company chains—the ability to react quickly to changes in the marketplace. The independents could be flexible in setting local prices (changing them daily or even hourly, if the need arose), an increasingly important consideration during the lean years of the Depression. The resultant price wars—and the resistance in some parts of the country to "outside" chains—convinced the oil companies to begin leasing stations to formerly salaried managers.

This interim step toward "true" franchising was solidified by two nearly simultaneous occurrences, which threatened to cost the oil companies millions of dollars based on the way they were then doing business: (1) Several states, beginning with Iowa, imposed license taxes on the oil companies, based on the number of stations a company operated; and (2) federal regulations began requiring businesses, including the chain operators, to pay Social Security taxes to the government and overtime wages to employees.

By the early 1930s, the petroleum marketers had become convinced of the effectiveness and potential savings of using local, nonemployee managers, and began granting franchises to these individuals (who, in many cases at first, were the former salaried managers of the stations). The franchisees benefitted from selling a nationally or regionally recognized brand of gasoline. The oil companies were able to maximize profits, not only by saving on employee salaries and taxes, but also by offering locally competitive prices and usually longer operating hours. The manager/franchisee's profit depended upon the profitability of the station—often resulting in a willingness to work longer hours.

These franchises proved so effective that by 1935, only a few years after they gained wide acceptance, they were by far the most popular way for a large petroleum company to sell gasoline nationally.

Thirsting for New Territory

Beginning in the late 1890s, the soft-drink industry followed a course somewhat parallel to the petroleum industry. At that time, a variety of beverages were bottled locally or were sold at soda fountains, with different cities or regions favoring different brands. Efficient nationwide distribution of soft drinks did not begin until franchising tenets were applied.

In 1899, two Chattanooga, Tennessee, businessmen obtained a license to bottle and distribute the Atlanta-based fountain drink, Coca-Cola. Under the terms of the license, Coca-Cola would sell the syrup for its soft drink to the bottler, and provide standardized labels and advertising support. The main stipulation of the license was that bottled Coke could not interfere with the company's soda-fountain sales.

Coke agreed to the franchise arrangement for three reasons: (1) It didn't make sense to centrally manufacture and then ship across the country (as opposed to manufacturing locally) a product that was mostly water; (2) they wanted to concentrate on the fountain business, believing that bottled soft drinks might be a "fad" and wouldn't amount to much; and (3) therefore, they wanted to avoid the capital requirements of building the regional plants it would take to economically produce their product. The end result was Coke obtained what it wanted—nationwide distribution of its product—without the capital outlay it would have taken to do it internally.

As the popularity of Coke increased, the pair of businessmen began granting contracts to far-flung operators who would locally bottle the soft drink from the syrup they purchased from the parent company. Within twenty years, there were more than one thousand Coca-Cola bottlers across the country. Other soft-drink brands—including Pepsi, Dr. Pepper, and Royal Crown—licensed their formulas to local bottlers in the early 1900s with similar, if not as wide-reaching, success. As with automobile and oil companies, many of the soft-drink companies which prospered over the last ninety years were the ones who began franchising early.

Franchising Evolves

The automobile, petroleum, and soft-drink industries, along with pioneering companies such as Singer Sewing Machine, turned to this form of franchising because they lacked efficient and affordable channels of distribution for their products. They could not afford to hire nationwide sales forces and corporately manage a spread-out chain. Instead, they sold the franchises to people who would take on the day-to-day responsibility—financially and operationally—of running these businesses.

And while these methods of product or tradename franchising were successful in spurring the use and growth of the franchise phenomenon, their progress began to slow after World War II. As we pointed out in Chapter 1, while this type of franchising still accounts for the majority of franchising revenues, the number of parent companies, individual outlets, and employees involved in it steadily declined in the postwar period. Meanwhile, changes in American society were setting the stage for the flowering of a different form of franchising.

The Birth of Business-Format Franchising

As the postwar era dawned, American society was changing. The baby boom resulted in a mass of young families; people moved in increasing numbers to the suddenly sprawling suburbs; and, more than ever, the automobile played a major part in everyday life.

In response to the growing needs of this emerging new society, restaurants specializing in quick take-out or eat-in meals started to proliferate. While most of these were local operations or regionalized mini chains, some nationally franchised chains such as A & W Root Beer, already existed. As these were joined in the 1950s by Burger King, Dunkin' Donuts, Dairy Queen, Burger Chef, Chicken Delight, and other national fast-food franchises, franchising was undergoing a subtle but important evolution.

Instead of simply granting a license to distribute or sell a product (as the practitioners of product franchising had done), the growing food franchises—joined by nonfood businesses such as Holiday Inn, Midas mufflers, and H & R Block—were employing a significantly different form of franchising. These franchisors sold the right to adopt an entire *business concept,* from recipes and uniforms to signs and advertising—often to licensees/franchisees with no previous experience in the given business. Although some business-format franchisors (as they came to be called) required franchisees to purchase certain usually proprietary supplies and products from them, their major source of income was payments for the use of their proven business system.

This was the rapidly changing business atmosphere Ray Kroc and McDonald's entered in the mid-1950s. Having observed burgeoning fast-food franchises as a traveling salesman, Kroc had assessed what he perceived to be the strengths and weaknesses of franchising, and used them as a guide in building McDonald's. The growth and success of business-format franchising are so closely intertwined with the success of its leading proponent— McDonald's—that no analysis of either would be complete without covering the other. By using business-format franchising to successfully create an empire built on franchised hamburger restaurants, Kroc effectively and permanently altered the way people and companies think about business expansion. And in these days of stagnation and decline in the U.S. auto and petroleum industries, it must be said that McDonald's has perhaps become the most *American* of all businesses. The phrase "As

American as apple pie" could well be amended to state "As American as *McDonald's*"!

Ray Kroc's Vision

While the public perception of Ray Kroc was and remains that of hamburger king and franchisor extraordinaire, he was, above all else, a master salesman. Kroc did not invent or start McDonald's. Nor did he invent fast food or business-format franchising. But he *did* refine each of them. He added his touch and vision to institutions and products that were good, perhaps even great, but not quite perfect.

The approach Kroc applied to franchising was as obvious (in retrospect) and revolutionary as the one Henry Ford had applied to the mass production of automobiles. And the two men and their companies realized identical results: fabulous success and a lasting impact on the socioeconomic structure of the United States—and, indeed, the entire world. (For a detailed history of Henry Ford, see Mancuso's book, *Running a Family Business,* Simon & Schuster, 1991.)

Kroc's Early Years

Kroc started searching for his niche early in life, dropping out of high school after his sophomore year and opening a music store to highlight his piano-playing skills. When World War I began, Kroc lied about his age to become an ambulance driver overseas. He was fifteen years old, and served in the same ambulance company as another underage driver who would later become world famous—Walt Disney.

After the war, Kroc put in a long stint peddling paper cups for Lily Cup Company. In the 1930s, he obtained the marketing rights to a multiple-spindle drink mixer called the Multimixer. He quit his job with Lily and started his own company to sell the new mixer, mainly targeting the restaurants and lunch counters that had previously been his paper-cup customers. His cross-country sales jaunts brought him into contact with a variety of food-service independents, chains, and even fledgling franchises, such as Tastee Freez and Dairy Queen. Although he was not a food-service professional, Kroc was an interested observer and was always studying his customers' businesses in order to better service their needs. As it turned out, this attentiveness to detail paid off just when Kroc needed it most. (It's a common entrepreneurial trait to be the most observant optimist—if not necessarily the brightest!)

Enter the McDonald Brothers

By the early 1950s, Multimixer sales had become stagnant, and it looked as though Kroc's company might fail. Then came a revelation. While most of Kroc's customers used only one Multimixer, with large lunch counters and ice cream stands perhaps having two, a hamburger stand in San Bernardino, California—run by brothers Dick and Mac McDonald—had recently purchased its *tenth* mixer and was using three or four at any given time.

At a loss to understand how a hamburger stand could need so many Multimixers (and hoping to pick up a few pointers to boost his sales), Kroc visited the brothers' stand in 1954. He was amazed to find masses of people standing in line to buy 15-cent hamburgers at the sales windows of a little octagonal building. As he watched workers efficiently serving the crowd, Kroc realized the minimal-menu, low-cost approach the brothers employed could easily—and probably successfully—be replicated.

In fact, the McDonald brothers had already begun franchising their so-called Speedy Service System—a handful of franchisees had purchased the rights to copy the name, menu, building, and general operating system of the successful original outlet. Kroc convinced the brothers to give him a chance as their new franchising agent, and McDonald's System, Inc., later renamed McDonald's Corporation, was born.

While Kroc's initial intention was to sell at least a pair of Multimixers to each new McDonald's franchise, he would soon realize that the real payoff could be in the restaurants themselves. While this may seem obvious in retrospect, it is an important point to keep in mind. To wit: How many entrepreneurs begin on the wrong horse, so to speak? And how many are self-confident enough to switch horses, as Kroc did? The moral of the story—for any businessperson—is not to be so "in love" with your concept or product that you fail to see a better application for it or a chance to radically and fundamentally improve upon it.

What Ray Kroc Did That Was Different

While Kroc was certain the brothers' concept of selling hamburgers was sound, he concluded the hands-off method they were using for franchising was seriously flawed. The first few McDonald's franchises were left more or less on their own after being provided with plans for their buildings and with details for implementing the Speedy Service System. Some were drastically changing the initial concept to suit their own ideas or tastes. Franchisees were even adding roast beef, hot dogs, tacos, and other items to the supposedly sacrosanct—and proven!—limited menu the brothers had perfected.

Kroc had come to realize from his days as a salesman, calling on various food-service franchises that the McDonald brothers' approach to franchising was pretty much the same one the rest of the crop of fledgling food-service franchisors were using. The franchisors would pitch the concept to potential franchisees, then issue rights and provide plans and manuals to anyone who could pay the franchise fee. Some would even offer a week or two of training to their new franchisees. However, this was often the last contact the franchisee had with the franchisor, who would move on to the next sales opportunity. Usually, these franchisors were more concerned with selling new franchises than with providing support or advice to existing franchisees.

In Kroc's view, these franchisors were taking a dangerously short-sighted approach to the expansion of their businesses. He thought they were committing slow suicide by not tending to the roots of their future success—the franchisees.

When Kroc took over the franchising of McDonald's, he was determined not to make the mistakes he had witnessed in other franchises. It was his firm belief that a franchisor's success depended on the success of its individual franchisees. His idea was to provide the franchisees with support, training, and the general business know-how to succeed. And he correctly surmised that as each franchisee prospered, the entire chain would grow stronger.

Making his franchisees happy and successful was no different to Kroc than what he had done when he was a paper-cup and Multimixer salesman. To him, both endeavors involved creating success by finding a way to make his product—be it cups or hamburger stands—become profitable for his customers, or, in the case of McDonald's, his franchisees. By basing the franchising of McDonald's on this simple and obvious approach, Ray Kroc transformed the eating habits of the world, and built McDonald's into the king of both fast food and franchising.

Franchising McDonald's

In 1955, Kroc opened his first McDonald's in Des Plaines, Illinois (just northwest of Chicago), using it from the beginning as a showcase for potential franchisees. (Today, that original store has been restored as a sort of McDonald's museum; customers eagerly inquiring about the 15-cent hamburgers advertised on the original sign are politely directed across the street to a modern McDonald's—featuring, alas, modern prices.) Two years later, there were thirty-seven McDonald's hamburger stands, mostly located in the widely dissimilar climes of southern California and the suburban Chicago area. It wouldn't be until 1968 that McDonald's introduced dine-in areas to its outlets on a wide scale.

In another two years, in 1959, the chain had reached the one-hundred-unit mark. Kroc was meticulously recreating, refining, and expanding the system he had discovered in the brothers' restaurant, and had begun to spread it across the country. While extensive amounts of time, effort, and money were devoted to perfecting and promoting the individual franchises, the parent company scraped by. To show his devotion to his new creation's vitally important formative years, Kroc drew no salary from McDonald's, instead living off a remaining trickle of Multimixer sales.

By 1961, the chain had grown to 228 units. That year, after many frustrations caused by the McDonald brothers' reluctance to accept the changes Kroc believed were necessary to ensure an even brighter future, Kroc bought out the brothers' share of the company—including continued use of their name—for $2.7 million. This sum was substantial for a parent company that had only shown $77,000 in profit the previous year, but the trade-off (and the debt incurred) was more than worth it for McDonald's Corporation—and was a dramatically bad deal in retrospect for Dick and Mac. They wanted a total of $2.7 million so each could clear a one-time windfall (after taxes) of $1 million. However, if the brothers had kept their 0.5 percent annual royalty on systemwide sales, it would be worth more than *$85 million a year* today!

Freedom To Grow

After the buyout, the company was free to head in any direction that Kroc wished. That direction was straight to the top. Nineteen sixty-nine saw the opening of the one thousandth McDonald's; only three years later, the total was two thousand. During this period, when McDonald's established itself as, then and since, the undisputed fast-food leader, Kroc slowly turned over much of the day-to-day control of the corporation to his trusted protégé, Fred Turner.

Kroc kept his hand in, making suggestions ranging from franchisee renewals to menu items. This last was never his forte; nearly all of the successful items McDonald's added to their menu, such as the Big Mac and Egg McMuffin, were developed by franchisees, rather than at the corporate headquarters. Growth continued at a steady pace—McDonald's unit total was more than five thousand by 1980.

Although Kroc's activities with McDonald's tapered off in the early 1980s, he gained further fame and publicity when he bought the San Diego Padres baseball team. Holding the title of senior chairman and founder, Kroc continued working full time for McDonald's until complications from two strokes landed him in a hospital for the months before his death in 1984.

In the decade of the 1980s, McDonald's more than doubled its number of units, reaching the seemingly unattainable total of ten thousand outlets around 1987. And the all-American golden arches have also reached *markets* that were once considered closed—the January 31, 1990, opening of the first McDonald's in the (then) Soviet Union caused great excitement in Moscow and a wealth of publicity both at home and abroad. Shortly after a grand opening that drew a systemwide record thirty thousand customers (spending the equivalent of $180,000 in Soviet rubles), the Moscow McDonald's had the highest level of sales of any McDonald's outlet. Remarkably, its daily totals have *increased* since opening day—some fifty thousand customers spend the equivalent of $300,000 in the Moscow McDonald's *every day*.

The Lesson of McDonald's

Ray Kroc understood hamburgers. But what he perhaps understood better than anything else is the following very important fact: *A franchise system cannot be completely successful until its franchisees achieve consistent levels of success.* That was why the major focus in the early years was on the individual stores rather than on the corporate structure. Simply put, Kroc and his original cadre of loyal corporate employees enriched their outlets before they enriched themselves. And, sure enough, those riches came later, along with the most stable, dynamic, and phenomenally successful franchise system ever created.

The First Franchising Boom

Perhaps the most significant sign of franchising's arrival as an accepted and desired form of business expansion occurred on April 15, 1965, when stock in McDonald's was first offered for sale in an I.P.O. (Initial Public Offering of stock). While traders and company executives munched hamburgers on the floor of the New York Stock Exchange, in a typical bit of well staged and widely covered McDonald's publicity, the stock was initially offered at

$22.50. Less than a month later, its value had doubled. And after twenty years the value of a single share of McDonald's stock had grown to approximately 175 times its initial offering price!

Soon after McDonald's stock went on sale, Holiday Inn and Kentucky Fried Chicken led other franchises in going public. For by the late 1960s those three national chains, and others such as Burger Chef, were nearing or had passed the one-thousand-unit mark. As the 1970s dawned, franchising—led most visibly by fast-food chains—had become assimilated into the American way of life *and* way of business. New franchises were springing up and quite often dying off practically overnight. Successes in the field included new categories of franchises (such as business and health services) or new businesses within proven categories. New entries in the fast-food arena, for example, included pizza parlors, Mexican restaurants, and other ethnic establishments.

Growing Pains—and Their Remedies

But everything was not completely rosy during the franchising boom years of the 1960s and 1970s. It became apparent the advantages of franchising could not overcome major fundamental flaws in a business concept or in the way a business was run. The aforementioned Burger Chef is a prime example. It started way ahead of McDonald's in number of units, and even in 1968, was still only a handful of outlets behind the future king of the hill. That year, however, Burger Chef was acquired by General Foods. Whether out of overcautiousness and an unfamiliarity with the market, or because (as they later asserted) the new management discovered that many of the restaurants were actually losing money, General Foods halted the expansion program. Soon after, Burger Chef began *losing* franchisees almost as quickly as it had been adding them previously. By the time General Foods unloaded the then-money-losing chain in the mid-1970s, it had fewer than three hundred outlets, down from a one-time high of 1,200.

Other highly publicized failures of this period included Minnie Pearl Fried Chicken restaurants (due to a lack of a solid operational format) and Arthur Murray's Dance studios, another franchise that traded heavily on a famous name and provided minimal support to franchisees. These and other failures and, occasionally, outright frauds, cheated investors and consumers alike and sullied the enviable record of success that franchising was building.

The backlash against franchising led to a degree of public contempt, even as that public continued to patronize franchised businesses in record numbers. One charge was that franchises were suspiciously inferior to local or independent businesses. This negative perception has faded in the intervening years, partially because the franchising industry itself realized a greater need for diligence in protecting its image and policing itself. At the same time, state and federal laws were enacted (with, for the most part, the support of the franchising industry) to guard against fraudulent or misleading practices in franchising. (We'll talk about some of those laws in more detail in Chapter 9.)

The overall state of the franchising industry *and* its public image today seem to have both reached an all-time high. However, even with franchising's huge success and acceptance, there are those who deride it as a plastic institution, void of personality. But the popularity of franchised businesses in general seems to indicate this group is in the minority. The overwhelming consensus seems to be, even with its occasional and attendant flaws, that franchising boasts a fascinating history and, more importantly, a prosperous present and a bright future.

Conversion Franchising
An Alternative Path

The late 1970s saw major growth in the third type of franchising we mentioned in Chapter 1 (after product franchising and business-format franchising): conversion franchising. Conversion franchises are exactly what their name implies—franchises converted from independents or small chains in the franchisor's line of business. While there have been examples of small-scale conversions in fast-food (the forty-plus-outlet Sandy's chain, an early copier of the McDonald's concept, was later converted to Hardee's franchises), hotels and motels, and other widely franchised businesses, the most successful efforts in the category occurred in the 1970s and early 1980s in a business that had previously experienced little franchising: real estate sales.

Franchising Finds a Home in Real Estate

In the mid- to late 1960s, Anthony Yniguez and his southern California–based Red Carpet Realty experienced the first large-scale success in converting independent real estate offices to franchises sharing a unified name. By offering the strength of advertising in a large region—and, eventually, nationally—along with training programs and a referral network, Red Carpet appealed to the sensibilities and the bottom line of independents. They saw that working together under one banner was more effective than competing as individual offices.

Another Californian, Art Bartlett, intensely studied Yniquez's approach and system and then "borrowed" it (as he fully admits) when he founded Century 21. Starting in 1971 with one office, the Century 21 chain grew impressively through conversion franchising to more than 7,500 offices by 1979. (That year, Century 21 was acquired in an exchange of stock with Trans World Corp.; it was sold to Metropolitan Life for more than $250 million in 1985.)

Conversion franchising has also been successfully applied to business services (such as accounting and temporary agencies), optometry (and other health care fields), hotels and motels, and the home remodeling and repair business.

Conversion: Pros and Cons

To broadly generalize, conversion franchising works best in a fragmented industry where no single organization has a strong regional or national identity. It gives franchisees greater marketing muscle, buying power, and, in some cases, an improved, streamlined business system.

The major drawback to conversion franchising in any field is the reluctance that many independent businesspeople feel when asked to subordinate the name of their business (which is, oftentimes, the businessperson's *own* name) and identity to that of a large franchised chain. This is especially difficult if the independents do not perceive a clear and present need or market advantage in doing so.

The New Boom: Franchising in the 1980s

The franchising boom of the sixties and seventies (and the various missteps and lessons it contained) gave way to an even stronger sustained boom of amazing growth during the 1980s and early 1990s. From 1980 to 1990, for example, franchising's annual sales figures grew from $336 billion to an estimated $716 billion—an increase of more than 113 percent. The number of new franchise outlets has also grown steadily, registering an increase of nearly 17 percent from 1980 to 1989.

The franchises that have successfully ridden this boom, prospering and proliferating in the last decade, are a disparate mix, ranging from frozen yogurt shops to quick-lube centers to employment agencies. Restaurants are still one of the most identifiable segments of franchising, but the trend is to more diverse and varied businesses, focusing on *specialties* rather than on broad categories.

Another major trend in franchised businesses that were born

and/or prospered in the last decade is the wide variety of service-oriented (rather than product-oriented) franchises, serving both personal and business needs. Examples include maid services, temporary personnel agencies, copy shops, equipment and appliance maintenance services, and many others.

Franchising Today

Franchising continues to grow, strongly and steadily. And the experts agree, barring major financial and/or sociological upheavals in the United States, that this growth should progress unabated.

To continue evolving and expanding in increasingly competitive fields, both new and old franchising companies are increasingly using any or all of the following three methods of starting out and/or staying strong.

New Concepts

When McDonald's was born, it was a new concept—a drive-in without carhops, with rock-bottom prices and fast service. And if it might seem that there are no more good ideas waiting to be developed, consider the video store. Based on a machine that became widely available to consumers only in 1980, video rental stores numbered approximately thirty thousand by 1990. And the biggest and best of those stores belonged to franchised chains, such as Blockbuster Video, National Video, and West Coast Video.

New Approaches

In fields that are not new, the next best thing to a new product or service is a new approach to that old product or service. Hamburgers are old hat, right? Not at Rally's, a drive-through-only hamburger chain that many believe could be one of the restaurant franchise successes of the 1990s. Rally's two "new" approaches are (1) confining its business to drive-through customers and (2) offering a limited, fourteen-item (as compared to sixty-plus currently for McDonald's) menu—itself reminiscent of the original McDonald's limited menu. The same holds true for Krystal, popular in the Southeast for their small, square hamburgers (similar to White Castle, but unlike White Castle, Krystal is aggressively expanding through franchising). Something old, something new, adding up to something potentially successful.

New Markets

If you've already gone everywhere, where do you go next? The seemingly contradictory answer is: you go someplace else. Some twenty to twenty-five years ago, as franchising began to boom and markets began to look crowded, many franchisors "risked" putting franchises in inner-city neighborhoods. Sure, there was trouble from time to time, but what emerged was joint franchisor/community benefits: a profitable market and vast pool of eager workers for the franchisor, and the opportunity for business ownership and employment for members of the community.

Today, similarly, those chains that have already blanketed the country, such as McDonald's, Kentucky Fried Chicken, Pizza Hut, and Subway, are looking beyond the United States for their next expansion challenge. Canada, England, Japan, Germany, the former republics of the Soviet Union, Mexico, and even China have become prime targets for U.S. franchisors. (We'll explore one of the hottest topics in this category, overseas franchising, in detail in our final chapter.)

Franchising's Journey: Short in Time But Long in Distance

In approximately thirty-five years, business-format franchising has grown from a handful of ice cream and hamburger stands into a multibillion-dollar industry encompassing scores of business categories. From 1980 to 1990 alone, business-format franchising has grown 50 percent faster than product franchising in sales, *and* has added establishments at a rate of more than 50 percent in the same period while the number of product establishments dropped by a quarter. (Conversion franchises can fall into either category—most, however, are business-format franchises—and are therefore not broken out as a separate statistical entity.) Approximately *three thousand* business-format franchisors operate in the United States—60 percent more than just ten years ago.

**DEVELOPMENT OF
THE TWO KINDS OF FRANCHISING:
"BUSINESS FORMAT" VS. "PRODUCT/TRADENAME"**

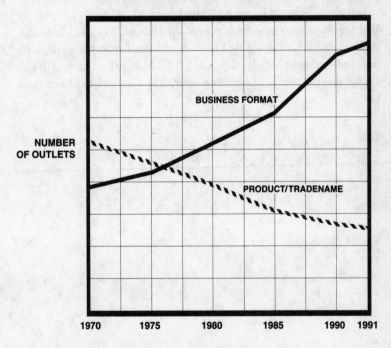

Franchising is still quite young compared to other methods of business expansion and marketing. Yet it already accounts for more than one-third of all U.S. retail sales. It is a way to start running your own business with the strength of hundreds or even thousands of successful outlets behind you. It can also help expand a local business into an international one.

In this chapter we have briefly examined what franchising is and how it works, and reviewed and analyzed its history. Those are two of the important goals this book set out to accomplish. Its next goals are to give specific, concrete help to potential franchisees and franchisors, answering questions and providing a clear picture of franchising.

In the next chapter, we will examine *you* as a potential franchisee. Do you have the "right stuff" to succeed as this special hybrid of employer and employee? A revealing self-test will help provide the important answer.

(Note: The chapters on franchisors begin with Chapter 7. But for those potential franchisors tempted to skip ahead, there's this caveat: The more you know about the concerns, goals, and personal makeup of the "typical" franchisee, the better a franchisor you will make. In other words, Ray Kroc would have read the franchisee chapters!)

Chapter Three

Becoming a Franchisee, Part I: Are You Qualified?

So, you want to become a franchisee?

Good idea!

We've already examined what franchising is and why it has grown to the proportions it has as a means of doing business. After such a buildup, we wouldn't blame you for wanting to rush out and start to look into becoming a franchisee.

But since it takes time and money to get into franchising, there's one very important question you have to ask yourself before you tackle this undertaking: Are you qualified to become a franchisee?

The immediate, prideful answer is likely to be, "Yes! I'm qualified to become *anything* I want to be!" That's a good, positive attitude—but while we're not impugning you or your abilities, we have to issue this caveat: Being a franchisee isn't necessarily for everyone. It isn't the same thing as owning a nonfranchised business; neither is it the same as working for someone else. Being a franchisee is a unique hybrid of both boss and employee—you own and run your franchised outlet, but you follow the system and dictates of the franchisor who has (presumably, anyway!) perfected the business. In return for the expertise, support, and established reputation you receive from the franchisor, you pay a percentage of your sales. In the best cases, this is a classic synergistic, win-win situation.

To be able to maintain the middle balance necessary to achieve success in this field, it takes a certain type of personality with very specific working traits and temperaments. What you probably are asking now is: What are these traits and do I have them?

In this chapter, we are going to examine these traits (and also deflate certain myths by showing you which traits mean very little as predictors of success). But first we are going to test your aptitude to become a franchisee.

Test Your Franchisee Aptitude

Joe remembers that Don used to say that during franchising's early days, before regulation helped clean up the acts of dubious franchisors, there were two basic and critical criteria for potential franchisees: the check test and the mirror test. First, did the franchisee's check clear the bank? And second, if you held a mirror under his nose, did it fog up, meaning the candidate was still breathing? Furthermore, Don joked, some franchisors didn't believe that the mirror test was that important, just as long as the check cleared!

Of course, this story exemplifies how much times have changed. Even if franchisee screening wasn't *that* loose and cynical back then, it sure has come a long way since. In fact, in the marketing and sales survey that we will cite extensively throughout this chapter (explained and described below), nearly *90 percent* of the franchisor respondents reported having rejected *financially qualified* franchisee applicants because of lack of other qualifications, which were judged to be more important to the long-term well-being of the franchise.

It is of no use to the stable, properly run franchisor to accept a franchisee merely because he or she can come up with the money; a franchise that eventually fails due to the choice of an unqualified franchisee costs the franchisor far more in time, money, and reputation than the quick, "easy" infusion of up-front money is ever worth. The days of the "check test" may not completely be history—there will always be unscrupulous operators (which is why it is important to thoroughly research franchisors)—but times *have* changed!

Today, franchisors obviously know what they want when it comes to franchisees, as demonstrated by the strong, very decisive responses to the aforementioned franchisor survey. And to help determine who does (or *doesn't*) have these traits, a growing number of franchisors—as also indicated by the survey results—have turned to some form of franchisee testing. How exactly do *you* measure up against the general traits that these franchisors are looking for?

To help answer this question, we have gathered some solid data. Don's company, Francorp, in association with DePaul University, has conducted extensive surveys of franchisors, gathering information from these sources on a number of topics regarding the marketing and sales of franchises. A special section of the most recent edition of this poll asked the franchisors to choose, from a list of two dozen, the traits they found to have been most important among their most successful franchisees. A total of 265 franchisors representing more than forty thousand franchised units responded to this survey.

Using these survey responses, and with the assistance of a clinical psychologist noted for his job-related diagnostic tests, we have created the following test to help prospective franchisees examine themselves as compared with the traits found in many of the most successful franchisees.

Are You Suited to Become a Successful Franchisee?

The following test for potential franchisees was specially prepared for this book with Dr. Harry E. "Bud" Gunn, Ph.D., a clinical psychologist. In addition to writing books and speaking on a variety of psychology-related topics, Dr. Gunn specializes in developing tests to assist various industries and corporations in hiring and evaluating personnel.

Starting with the raw data from the Francorp/DePaul franchisor's survey, this diagnostic test was created based on the responses to that survey. In order to determine your potential for success as a franchisee, answer each question to the best of your ability. The test will be most useful if you answer each question as accurately as you can in terms of your own feelings and experiences, rather than providing the answer that you *think* a candidate should provide to be a successful franchisee.

Remember, this test is designed to measure your aptitude to be a *franchisee,* not your worth as a person or your overall general business acumen. As we have noted, the life and career of a franchisee is not for everyone, and it is important to find out if it is right for you before investing considerable time and money to explore specific options within franchising.

(Before you take this test, you may wish to obtain a copy of a similar profile, "Do You Have What It Takes to Be an Entrepreneur?", which was developed several decades ago by Joe through his organization, The Center for Entrepreneurial Management [CEM]. This twenty-six-question "Entrepreneur Quiz" has been very popular and has appeared in *Playboy, Penthouse,* and a host of other publications. It was developed by Joe in a similar manner to this franchise test from data gathered from about three thousand dues-paying members of CEM. The profiles of the two types—franchisees and entrepreneurs—are, as you may imagine, quite different. For a copy, send $10 to: Joe Mancuso, The Center for Entrepreneurial Management, Inc., 180 Varick Street, Penthouse, New York, NY 10014, 212-633-0060, fax 212-633-0063.)

The *Only* Franchisee Test You Need to Take!

For questions 1–16, please circle the answer that *best* describes you
or that you *most agree* with (depending on what the question asks).

1. I have generally been regarded as:
- a. one who loves to plan vacations.
- b. always being willing to work hard.
- c. one who seeks benefits and rewards for my work.
- d. being easy to supervise.

2. Financially, I:
- a. am very conservative.
- b. am very liberal.
- c. have always been able to put money aside.
- d. have never been well off.

3. Taking directions from others is:
- a. one of my strong talents.
- b. something I do not like.
- c. often a must.
- d. acceptable if not constantly required.

4. Work-related pressure:
- a. can cause physical illness.
- b. is something I try to avoid.
- c. is a definite problem in business today.
- d. seldom causes me any discomfort.

5. I have generally been regarded as having:
- a. the ability to sell things.
- b. a good grasp of "what makes people tick."
- c. physical strength.
- d. emotional warmth.

6. To reach one's optimum level of success, one must:
- a. have luck on his or her side.
- b. be happy in his or her work.
- c. be willing to take risks.
- d. know the right people.

7. Personally, I:
   a. am dissatisfied with my current profession.
   b. have had a variety of life experiences.
   c. have strong business and sales skills.
   d. have not had much business experience.

8. A major factor in business success is:
   a. an appetite to learn more about what you do.
   b. a happy and stable personal life.
   c. physical stamina.
   d. extensive business experience.

9. I am *best* described as:
   a. an intelligent person.
   b. a highly verbal person.
   c. a hard-driving person.
   d. a person who can relate to other people.

10. A strong desire to learn is:
   a. a valuable asset, both personally and professionally.
   b. often necessary to advance in business.
   c. not very important once you complete school.
   d. uncommon in the business world.

11. When a superior tells me what to do, I:
   a. wish I had his job so I could give orders.
   b. often try to present a new, more efficient way of doing the task.
   c. secretly resent being ordered around.
   d. learn from the instructions and complete the task.

12. To succeed in business, it is often more important to be hard-working than to be a creative, talented person.
   a. I strongly agree.
   b. I agree.
   c. I disagree.
   d. I strongly disagree.

13. I have been *best* known for:
   a. getting involved in my community.

    b. having good general business knowledge and skills.
    c. being a good parent.
    d. my work experience with a large company organization.

14. As a business owner, it would be most important to me to:
    a. provide jobs to my family.
    b. be well thought of by my staff.
    c. be able to set my own work schedule.
    d. be closely aware of and prudent with my finances.

15. Work hours should be:
    a. as long as is needed.
    b. paid for, especially for the boss.
    c. flexible—long only when needed for special projects.
    d. equally divided among all employees.

16. A description of someone with a good chance to succeed in business is someone who:
    a. likes to regularly get away to help avoid stress.
    b. is always curious to learn more about doing her job.
    c. works best by himself.
    d. has a business degree from a top university.

For questions 17–30, pick the statement that *best* describes you.

17.   a. I have a strong affinity for sales.
     b. I am highly energetic.

18.   a. I have moderate experience in the type of business I would like to get into.
     b. I am a good direction-taker.

19.   a. I am a creative person.
     b. I am a good listener.

20.   a. I am a previous business owner.
     b. I am able to fully commit my finances to my business.

21.   a. I don't mind working long hours.
        b. I have strong corporate skills.

22.   a. I am a very careful, organized person.
        b. I am a people-oriented person.

23.   a. I am a charitable person.
        b. I am a diplomatic person.

24.   a. I am highly spontaneous.
        b. I am highly goal-directed.

25.   a. I am able to take charge of people.
        b. I am a quick decision-maker.

26.   a. I have some basic financial knowledge.
        b. I have previous management experience.

27.   a. I need to be in control.
        b. I can take directions from others.

28.   a. I have extensive business skills.
        b. I am always willing to do what it takes to get things done.

29.   a. I often use weekends to unwind after the workweek.
        b. I am very resistant to stress.

30.   a. I have money in the bank.
        b. I am willing to do without if necessary.

31. For this question, circle the five following statements that are *least* like you:
    a. I am a slow starter.
    b. I am able to sell anything.
    c. I prefer to work by myself.
    d. I am interested in learning new skills.
    e. I would rather live spontaneously than set long-range goals.
    f. I thrive on stressful, busy, deadline situations.
    g. I work best by taking charge and issuing orders.

h. I am rich in people skills.

i. I prefer a large corporate environment.

j. I have a history of working long hours at favorite activities.

Scoring

For each answer you have chosen, give yourself the corresponding amount of points listed below:

1. a-0, b-4, c-0, d-2

2. a-2, b-0, c-4, d-0

3. a-4, b-0, c-2, d-1

4. a-0, b-0, c-1, d-4

5. a-4, b-2, c-0, d-0

6. a-0, b-2, c-4, d-0

7. a-0, b-2, c-4, d-0

8. a-4, b-1, c-0, d-3

9. a-1, b-0, c-2, d-4

10. a-4, b-2, c-0, d-0

11. a-0, b-2, c-0, d-4

12. a-4, b-3, c-0, d-0

13. a-0, b-4, c-2, d-1

14. a-1, b-0, c-0, d-4

15. a-4, b-0, c-2, d-0

16. a-0, b-4, c-1, d-1

17. a-2, b-1

18. a-1, b-2

19. a-1, b-2

20. a-1, b-2

21. a-2, b-1

22. a-1, b-2

23. a-1, b-2

24. a-1, b-2

25. a-2, b-1

26. a-2, b-1

27. a-1, b-2

28. a-1, b-2

29. a-1, b-2

30. a-2, b-1

31. a-1, b-0, c-1, d-0, e-1, f-0, g-1, h-0, i-1, j-0

TOTAL POINTS POSSIBLE: 97

Ratings

97–79 points: A Prime Candidate. Congratulations! If you have answered the quiz questions frankly and received a score in this range, your personality traits, attitude, experience, and temperament are good matches with the attributes many franchisors say are found in their most successful franchisees. You likely have a well defined desire to learn and a willingness to follow directions in the quest for your own success. If you are financially able to do so, we strongly suggest that you pursue becoming a franchisee. Good luck!

79–50 points: A Potential Candidate. Many of your traits are close to those found in top franchisee candidates; however, you may not be *completely* committed to the concept of running a franchised outlet of someone else's business. Although you may be definitely interested in becoming a franchisee, your quiz answers indicate you might have some differences in opinion as compared with more "traditional" candidates; perhaps you have a strong streak of independence or are more comfortable giving directions than taking them. If you can ascertain those areas in which you differ from the "model franchisee"—by reading the following section analyzing important traits—you may be able to determine if these are fundamental differences (which may mean that franchising *isn't* for you) or are merely slight discrepancies. If the latter is true, you, too, could turn out to be a good franchisee candidate.

50–0 points: A Questionable Candidate. A low score on this test might simply indicate that you would be more comfortable and successful as an independent business owner or as an employee of an independent business or a large corporation. Becoming a franchisee is not for every personality type; you may be more independent and have a stronger business background than most franchisees. Rather than trying to squeeze your individual talents into a field for which you may not be suited, you should probably seek other opportunities. If you still feel you are strongly committed to becoming a franchisee, examine the choices you made on the test that differ from the suggested answers. Doing this can show you which areas in your personality or background you need to reassess to improve your chances at becoming a successful franchisee. Read on, and we will closely examine those traits—and show you which ones *are* and *aren't* judged to be important to success as a franchisee.

Traits of Successful Franchisees

What does it take to make a successful franchisee? How do your own skills, desires, and experiences compare to those found among a sampling of the most successful franchisees extant? For example, how important is it to have previous experience in the franchisor's field, or to have previously worked for a large corporation? What are the most common traits that franchisors are looking for in prospective franchisees?

We will now examine both the *most* and *least* important of these franchisee traits—as determined by respondents to the Francorp/DePaul franchisors' survey.

The Most Important Traits

The following were the most highly rated traits; most of the respondents judged each of the following characteristics to be "critical" to a franchisee's success.

Eagerness to Learn

More than three-quarters of the survey's respondents chose this trait as critical—making it the highest-rated, and, one could conclude, the most important attribute many franchisors look for among prospective franchisees. This comes as little surprise, since, in effect, franchising can be boiled down to two tasks: teaching and systematization. (These words obviously oversimplify the matter, but the point is still valid.) Franchisors teach their franchisees how to run the business (or, in the case of conversion franchises, franchisors teach their franchisees a *modified*—and, presumably, an improved—way of doing business); these "students" must then repeat their lessons over and over as they serve their customers. Therefore, it follows that an eagerness to learn would serve a franchisee well. This eagerness to learn is not necessarily to be confused with having an education; although it is a definite advantage to have a high school education, and at least *some* amount of college can be helpful, less than 10 percent of those franchisors replying said that *any particular level* of formal education was a critical requirement.

Willingness to Work Long Hours

The fact that more than two-thirds of all respondents identified this as a critical trait clearly underscores the point that there is no easy road to success in business ownership. Simply put, franchisees who want to succeed can expect, especially in the early days of running their units, to work long and hard hours to make their businesses successful. In other words, you will have little or *no* staff to rely upon (expect, perhaps, unpaid family members)—quite a different situation from the backgrounds of most corporate executives. Franchisors require this sort of devotion from their franchisees, and prospective franchisees who are willing and aware of this have a better chance of making it than those who may be less committed to taking on a new, large workload. It's definitely a case of perspiration, not inspiration.

Highly Developed "People Skills"

Franchisees have to artfully and diplomatically deal with suppliers, employees, franchisor personnel, and, most importantly, their customers. To best do so, franchisees need to be able to express themselves, to listen, and to have patience in dealing with a variety of situations. Accordingly, franchisors look for individuals who are at least somewhat outgoing, communicative, and able to instill confidence in those around them. We can't stress enough the need for an ability to listen. The good news is that this skill, as rare as it may be, can be taught. Remember—God gave us all two ears and only one mouth.

Sales Ability

Whether it is pizzas, pets, or paint jobs, every franchise sells something. And while you need not be a master salesperson to survive or succeed as a franchisee, you *will* need at least *some* level of sales ability. In a way, the evaluation of this ability will likely start the instant you meet with a franchisor, including the way you present yourself, the way you enumerate your skills, and the way you handle their questions. In other words, the franchisor will evaluate how you "sell" yourself. Again, this is a skill that can be learned—just notice how many sales seminars are conducted every year.

Resistance to Stress

It's your twelfth straight hour working at your franchised outlet. The phone is ringing, a customer's baby is crying, an employee needs you to handle a dispute with an irate customer, and you're behind on getting your required paperwork filled out and sent to the franchisor's headquarters. A bad day? Sure, but it could be *any* day in the life of a new franchisee. Especially during the period before running your franchise becomes second nature, you are likely to face some trying and stressful days (and nights!). Can your temperament handle these situations? Can you focus on necessary tasks, no matter what distractions and/or deadlines accompany them? Franchisors know that being a franchisee is often stressful, which is why they will want to know how well you handle stress. (This is another skill that can be learned and probably should be by most businesspeople!)

Ability to Take Directions

Similar to "eagerness to learn" (yet with a subtle difference), this trait was rated as critical by more than half of those franchisors who responded to the survey. In franchising, faith and trust must be placed in the methods the franchisor has developed; directions and requirements are not made capriciously, but rather to benefit the franchisee and the rest of the franchise system. Consequently, franchisees must be able to subordinate many of their personal opinions and desires to those of the franchisor. For example, an unyielding "my way or the highway" type of person who chafes at taking suggestions or orders is not a good candidate to become a successful franchisee.

Having Money in Reserve

More than 90 percent of respondents rated this trait as either critical or at least somewhat important to the success of a franchisee. This may contradict the common perception of a franchisee who has his "last dime" invested in his business (and, therefore, in himself), but it just makes good business sense. Yes, franchisors want their franchisees to be committed, personally and financially, to the success of their units. But they also want the franchisee to be able financially to weather any hard times, either early on in the life of a particular unit or during an uncontrollable economic downturn. A franchisee with some money in reserve will be better able to deal with any hard times that may be encountered.

The Least Important Traits

The highly rated traits noted above give you a better idea of what most franchisors are looking for in franchisees. But, conversely, what traits are *not* important to franchisors? We've also identified those attributes—and some of them may surprise you. The following traits were judged to be "irrelevant" to a franchisee's potential for success by most of the franchisors who replied to the survey.

Experience Working for a Big Company

Nearly 85 percent of the respondents said this trait had nothing to do with whether a franchisee could be successful in their system (in comparison, only *2 percent* rated this as being critical). While most franchisors have a number of franchisees who have bailed out (or been euphemistically "outplaced") of corporate life, in no way do these franchisors place much importance on this background.

Previous Experience in the Franchisor's Field

Most of the franchisors surveyed downplayed the importance of prior experience in their line of business. In fact, over the years we have seen many franchisors who would much prefer to deal with franchisees who have *no* experience in their field. The franchisors often feel that it is easier to train these novices than it is to *retrain* someone with preexisting ideas and habits (i.e., ideas and habits *contrary* to those of the franchisor).

Prior Business Ownership (or Lack Thereof)

This trait was posed as both a positive and a negative—for example, "Are franchisees who have previously owned their own business more likely to be successful as a franchisee?" and "Are franchisees who have *not* previously owned their own business more likely to be successful as a franchisee?" Perhaps surprisingly, neither condition rated very highly among franchisors. With the obvious exception of conversion franchisees, franchisors are neither specifically looking for people who have owned their own businesses, nor are they systematically seeking to exclude these people. Franchisors feel that *some* level of prior business experience can be helpful, but the degree of this experience is far less important in the development of a successful franchisee than (for example) an eagerness to learn and an ability to follow directions.

Personal Situations (Age, Sex, and Marital/Family Status)

Conventional wisdom would probably dictate that most franchisors would prefer middle-aged, married males with a family as franchisees because, perhaps, members of this group are usually regarded as being responsible individuals with vested interests in succeeding (i.e., to support their families). However, respondents to this survey indicated that age, sex, marital status, and family situations seem to mean little when it comes to predicting future franchisee success; the percentage who consider these "irrelevant" were as follows: age, 59 percent; sex, 79 percent; marital status, 71 percent; and family status, 62 percent. It must be noted these questions were not qualified—for example, the question simply inquired if the sex of a franchisee matters, *not* if the franchisor preferred males over females or vice versa.

63

Financial Acumen

Did you often doze off during Accounting 101? Not to worry. The total of franchisor respondents who judged this characteristic to be either irrelevant or only somewhat important to a franchisee's success was more than 77 percent. Some knowledge of basic accounting and reporting conventions *can* be helpful, but whatever financial routines are needed will likely be taught by the franchisor; standardized accounting, banking, and other financial procedures will be part of the operating system provided. In general, franchisors are looking for enthusiastic, committed, quick learners, not necessarily CPAs.

Other traits that the survey inquired about were judged to be neither absolutely critical nor completely irrelevant by the franchisors who responded. These include general physical fitness, creativity, participation in community affairs, management experience (i.e., previously overseeing a staff, an outlet, or an entire business) or other specialized business skills, and a willingness to take risks.

Now that you know which traits are valued most by franchisors in successful franchisees—and which traits mean relatively little—you should have a clearer picture of where *you* stand in regard to them. You also have a better idea of why you scored the way you did on the quiz (whether it was a high or low score). Perhaps, especially if you were disappointed with your score, you could benefit from looking over the test questions again, analyzing your responses as they compare to what you now know is important to a franchisor.

If, even after doing so, you realize that you may *not* be prime franchisee material but would still like to become your own boss, we recommend reading Joe Mancuso's bestseller, *How to Start, Finance, and Manage Your Own Small Business* (Fireside/Simon & Schuster, 1986). This classic has been reprinted ten times and contains the Entrepreneur's Quiz (mentioned earlier in this chapter), which allows you to measure your entrepreneurial potential against the three thousand members of Joe's organization, The Center for Entrepreneurial Management, Inc. Even if you've determined that franchising isn't for you, we wish you luck with your own entrepreneurial pursuits!

The Next Step

Now that you have a better idea of how you rate, personally and professionally, as a prospective franchisee, the next step on your journey is to begin evaluating franchises toward the ultimate decision of choosing a franchise organization with which to cast your lot. Of course, the franchisor that you choose must also choose *you,* but if you're pleased with your test score and if you feel the traits described above dovetail nicely with your personality and experiences, you have a good chance of appealing to many franchisors as a possible franchisee.

We now move on to the large but very important task of separating the franchising wheat from the chaff!

Becoming a Franchisee, Part II: Narrowing Your Choices

Have you ever known someone—a relative, a friend, a business associate—who drives by a McDonald's and says, "See that McDonald's? In 1960 (or '65 or '70 or '75 or *whatever*) I could've had that for a song"?

This person will go on to tell you he or she could have bought a McDonald's franchise back then for $25,000 (or whatever the amount might be), but today you had better have $450,000 to $650,000 available—and that's *if* you can get one.

True enough. Anybody could be rich today with the help of a time machine. All you'd have to do is go back and buy Xerox at 2 or bet on the upset Jets to win Super Bowl III or sign up for one of Ray Kroc's first franchises. (But considering many of today's "shrewd" businesspeople, someone would probably go back, leverage Kroc out of control of the company, and promptly run McDonald's into the ground, undoubtedly altering the future history of the world!)

But that drive-by story brings one moral to mind: Do *you* want to drive past some thriving franchise (perhaps a franchise that is just starting out today) in ten or twenty years and say, "That could've been *mine*"?

Anyone could make a good decision about *today* if she could look back with the accumulated advantage of twenty years or so of hindsight. Needless to say, the best and most beneficial time to make a good decision about today—and about the future—is *now*. And that's what this chapter is about: beginning the process of making your decision about which franchise to buy.

Now that you know what it takes to become a successful franchisee—and have a better idea how well suited your talents and experience are to this endeavor—the next stage is to get a handle on exactly which franchise you would like to buy. And if this sounds like a daunting task (even for those with a general idea of the field they want to go into), it's because it *is*. The total number of franchisors out there is already in the thousands and is growing by hundreds every year. Where do you even begin?

Why, right here, of course! In this chapter, we'll help you navigate your way through the oft-perilous seas of choosing a franchise. We'll size up how much risk you're prepared to take. We'll pit your logic against your emotion and see which is dominant. We'll show you how to be four to eight years ahead of potentially lucrative trends. And we'll let you know what kinds of franchises you should *definitely* avoid.

Finding the "Perfect" Franchise

Having seen our lists in Chapter 1, you may be wondering, "Which one of those is the right franchise for me?" We'll help you determine at the very least which of some of those lists you *might* choose from (except, of course, the "Glue Factory" list!).

You may also be wondering if, at the end of this chapter, we will have narrowed down the choices for you and will make a suggestion for the "perfect" franchise (or franchises) to buy. Remember the old adage about if you give a man a fish, he'll eat for a day, but if you teach a man to fish, he'll never go hungry again? Telling you which franchise you should buy would be like giving you a fish and, even with our experience and expertise in the field, by the time you read any individual suggestion we could make . . . well, you know what happens to a fish past its prime.

On the other hand, if we show you how to intelligently weigh all of the factors involved and make the choice best suited to your abilities and background, we've instead shared our fishing experience. And, after all, it *should* be your decision; our goal is simply to help better prepare you to make it. So bait up your hook and prepare to cast your line into the well-stocked waters of franchising.

(At this point, you may be thinking, "But I already *know* what franchise I want to buy." If so, fine—we're not trying to talk you out of anything. But we do suggest that you read on to see the important component parts that should go into such a decision. It may reinforce your choice—or help you reevaluate it.)

How Not to Become a Franchisee

Before we start examining the factors that go into a well-rounded decision on how to become a franchisee, we need to run through approaches or attitudes we feel can be detrimental to the process. Here, then, are three ways *not* to become a franchisee.

Don't Rely on Brokers
While we *do* strongly suggest you solicit the advice of experts (such as lawyers, accountants, and qualified consultants) when the time is appropriate, we don't feel your best interests are served by abdicating your research or your decision making to others. There

are a variety of brokers and agents who may or may not have your best interests in mind when it comes to making a business decision—so why entrust your future to their hands? The field of franchise consulting has many well-established companies and individuals, but for the most part these consultants best help people become *franchisors*. We heartily endorse use of reputable consultants for *that* process (see Chapter 8), but as for becoming a franchisee, it's *your* money, *your* life, and *your* future. Be sure to make it *your* decision!

Don't Look to Get Rich Quick

This was part of our general advice about franchising for both franchisees *and* franchisors (see Chapter 1), but we feel it's important enough to repeat. The perception of franchising as a "license to print money" arose during the first franchising boom of the 1960s and was reinforced during the last decade or so—but as any experienced person knows, there is no sure thing in business. (Remember, when a person with experience meets a person with money, the person with money usually gets experience—and vice versa!) Yes, franchising has an enviable record of success, but it's not magic. By making a carefully informed decision and backing it up with dedicated hard work, you *can* make a successful go of franchising. Just understand that, as in any business endeavor, your success is not *guaranteed*.

Don't Try to Get into Franchising "On the Cheap"

As we said in the beginning of Chapter 3, it's going to take time and money to get into franchising. Perhaps we should have said "it takes time and money to get into franchising *intelligently*." Choosing a franchise is a complex decision that requires a "critical mass" of time and money. Thinking you can do it cheaply by cutting corners and collapsing timeframes can be potentially disastrous.

Those caveats stated, we will cover the *right* way to start the process of choosing a franchise.

Assessing and Setting Your Objectives

As with any important venture, as you enter franchising, you need to identify your desires and goals. After taking the test in the previous chapter, you should have a better sense of whether becoming a franchisee is right for you. But there's more you need to consider. What sort of fields do you know or are interested in? Do you want to be in a field you know and have experience in or do you want to try something new? Do you want to simply (in effect) buy yourself a job? Do you want to establish something you can pass on to your children? Do you want to be a sort of mini-entrepreneur, owning more than one franchise or an entire franchise territory? Are you interested more in the long or the short term? Do you want a proven franchise or more of a long shot with a potentially larger payoff?

Knowing the answers will help you narrow your choices. As you examine various industries or individual franchises, you will have personal objectives against which to measure them. But at this point your single most important consideration should be, How much risk am I willing to take?

(In later stages of consideration, financial matters—investment, rates of return, potential income, etc.—are another very important consideration. We cover that phase of the process in the following chapter.)

The Risk Continuum

The very fact that you are considering buying a franchise means you want less risk than is involved in starting an independent business.

You are looking at getting into a business with the advantages of a proven operating system, ongoing support, and wide-ranging (perhaps even national) advertising. But even within the generally less risky context of franchising, varying levels of risk exist—and tied to these levels of risk are the price they will cost you and the level of potential return they can generate. This relationship can be illustrated by the chart below:

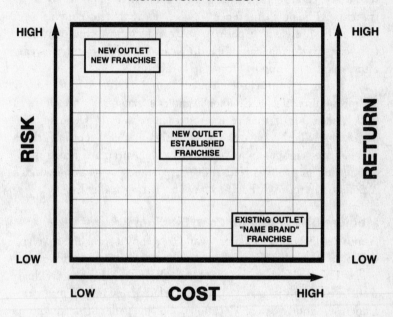

RISK/RETURN TRADEOFF

The three points on this continuum represent convenient touchstones in the intertwined relationship of the elements of risk, cost, and return. Countless gradations could represent variances in any individual element or in all three. But to give you a general idea of the elements involved, we will describe three demarcations.

Low Risk, High Cost, Low Return

To minimize your risk (but maximize your cost), you could buy an existing, operating, proven franchise outlet. Even if you succeed, you won't make a fortune, but your likelihood of making money *at all* will be significantly increased. (How much should you expect to make, whatever your level of risk? This important consideration is covered in depth in the next chapter.) And, considering the probable cost of such a blue-chip franchise, you are likely to have to lay out a substantial amount of cash or take on a substantial amount of debt.

Of course, if that route is your choice, franchising is really secondary. You're just buying a business that happens to be a franchise. The only difference between doing that and buying any existing business is that perhaps you can feel more confident that last year's performance will be duplicated next year and the year after, thanks to support from the franchisor.

If this is your chosen course, simply refer to our list of "Thoroughbreds" (see Chapter 1) and call franchisees in your own backyard to see if they're interested in selling. (Of course, the *franchisors* will also have their say in this matter—typically, they will have the right to approve any such sale. And many franchisors retain the right of first refusal over any franchise resales, making it potentially more difficult to buy an existing franchise.)

Medium Risk, Medium Cost, Medium Return

A more risky course of action would be to buy a franchise that has less of a blue-chip aura—with an accompanying reduction in price. The three elements that generally establish an individual franchise outlet's level of risk are the relative newness of industry, franchise, and market (location). So in general, a medium risk/cost/return franchise would have some elements of relative newness to one or more of those three categories.

As with any gray area (as opposed to the black and white extremes at the ends of the continuum), the middle can get a little murky. For example, what is riskier—a brand-new franchise in an established industry in an emerging market or an established franchise in an emerging industry in a new market? And conjecture continues through all of the possible permutations. In general, however, in this range you'll be risking more than with the blue chippers, with a corresponding drop in price but with a potentially higher return.

High Risk, Low Cost, High Return

Following the continuum to its logical end, we come to the riskiest—and, potentially, the most lucrative—type of franchise.

In other words, these franchises represent a relatively high degree of newness in all three categories. (And, of course, theoretically, the riskiest franchise would be a completely new franchise in a completely new industry in a completely new market.)

If you're up to the challenge of this kind of franchise, check our list of up-and-coming "Dark Horses" (see Chapter 1), and make calls to see if entire franchise *territories* are available. Even if you hadn't considered taking on a franchise territory (which makes you sort of a hybrid between a franchisee and franchisor), if you're willing to take on a high level of risk, the rewards of territory development can be more than worth it.

For example, when Blockbuster Video started out, it was a considerable risk. It stocked more than five times the number of tapes than regular video stores and it was capital-intensive and expensive for an unproven concept. But those who bought territories early on benefitted greatly (some to the tune of up to ten times their initial investment) by developing and eventually selling the territory back to the parent company.

Once you have an idea where you want to fall on the risk continuum, you can assess the other major factor that will likely steer your decision in the early stages: emotion.

Emotion: The Immeasurable Factor

Now that we've established the risk/return relationship, imagine a two-dimensional graph, with risk/return (from low to high) as the vertical axis. We say "imagine," because this is not a graph you can actually plot lines on—but you *can* learn from it.

The reason for the imaginary status of this graph is that, when considering a franchise, the horizontal axis would be labeled "Emotion," an immeasurable and unpredictable factor; it's simply impossible to plot emotion on a linear scale. No matter what logic dictates, there will always be someone who says, "Risk, schmisk. I want a pizza franchise because I've always wanted to spin that dough in the air" or "I want that lawn-care franchise because I've always wanted to work outside all day" or whatever it is you've always wanted to do.

Basically, it can be said there are two kinds of potential franchisees: (1) those interested in getting into the *franchising* business, and (2) those interested in getting into the chicken or oil-change or *whatever* business. This is not to say that one is better than the other. Looking at the entire field of franchising may be more logical, but we realize the emotional attraction of one particular field or franchise often can be strong.

In Chapter 1, we told you about Joe's brother, John, who bought a Physicians Weight Loss Center franchise after he lost sixty pounds as a customer at his local franchise. He didn't know diet centers or weight-loss plans, but he *did* know he lost more than 20 percent of his total body weight, so he got into the business. But as we hinted before, the results were disastrous. And this is not an isolated example.

Executives in Don's company recently had occasion to talk to executives from Popeye's Famous Fried Chicken in New Orleans. They have some seven hundred units and recently acquired Church's Fried Chicken, with another 1,200 or so units. They were asked about the common denominators of their typical franchisees. The response: "We've got doctors, lawyers, bankers, families, husbands and wives, young professionals, etc. But the real common factor is most of them were first interested in becoming franchisees because they like the chicken." Popeye's also said a recent franchisee of theirs was a perfect example of this phenomenon. This gentleman is a doctor who went to college in New Orleans. He liked the chicken back then, but his current practice is in a town without a Popeye's. He missed it and said, "I guess I'm gonna have to buy a franchise in order to have this chicken." So he did! Such is the power of emotion in the franchise-buying process.

(A famous example of emotion in corporate business is the Victor Kiam/Remington story. Kiam's wife bought him a Remington razor, he liked it, and he bought the company. However, we have no explanation of why Kiam also bought the New

England Patriots football team, which has compiled some embarrassing win-loss records in the last few seasons.)

The Danger of Liking the Chicken

Early in a franchise program, many franchisees tend to be customers of the particular business. The scenario is fairly straightforward: The customer is happy with the product or service, makes an inquiry as to its availability, and ends up purchasing a franchise. Oftentimes, risk/return decisions are not huge factors in these purchases—the customer simply likes the business, assumes that other people will like it, and buys in. (Perhaps we've got you thinking about some business that you frequent and like—"I wonder if they franchise" or "I wonder if that franchise is available in my area?" The only way to find out is to ask!)

However, there is a danger of falling in love with your product: You love this chicken, but will everyone else? Or "I love this pizza"—but is the field saturated (in your area or nationwide—whatever market you're looking at)? Don't fall into the trap of romanticizing the business beyond its actual proportions. Remember, it's a business transaction: You're buying a franchise, not a pizza or a T-shirt or a service you liked. Are there enough *other* people who will like it? Is the market growing or shrinking? You like the chicken, sure; but to put it bluntly, do you like the chicken enough to eat it for *every meal* if your franchise isn't making money?

This reminds us of the old joke about the banker who said, "I only lend money to liquor stores, because I know in the worst case I can drink my way out of the problem!"

Emotion versus Logic

As we said, risk/return is highly measurable and emotion is immeasurable. In the best-case scenario (or, at least, the most *logical* scenario), if emotion is removed from the buying process, you can choose the type of franchise that's best for your desired level of risk/return.

Logical as you may be, however, you can never fully remove emotion from a decision that large. Let's face it—many of life's major decisions have little to do with pure logic. For example, if you looked at getting married and having children in a strictly logical manner, you'd say, "It costs too much, it's too much hassle, can I change my life-style that much?" But emotionally, it's "I love you, let's get married, let's buy a house, let's have kids." We know that marriages fail, houses cost too much, and having kids puts a strain on your time and money—but based on emotional appeal, we do these things and will keep doing them.

Our goal here is to give you the analytical tools to work things out for yourself when it comes to choosing a franchise. We know you're still going to add your own emotions into the mix, but if you know the score, if you consider the details logically as well as emotionally, you can at least minimize your chance of failure. In other words, don't be afraid to let your emotions come into play—but be aware that you're doing it and don't let your ultimate decision be *purely* emotional. Your goal should be to strike that delicate balance between "This is the amount of risk I'm comfortable with" and "I like the chicken!"

Furthermore, as the process progresses, you will need to become even more analytical. There will come a stage—covered in the next chapter—where you will need to weigh your choices from a standpoint of investment (of money and time) and return on that investment. Again, we will help you to best make that decision by highlighting the factors you should be considering.

Where Logic and Emotion Meet

If you were to approach the concept of picking a franchise in the most logical way possible, you would first choose the industry and then you'd narrow down available franchises within that industry.

But, of course, this rarely happens. It is much more common for potential franchisees to look at franchises in a number of different industries. This is a *horizontal* search, cutting across various franchises in various industries, rather than a *vertical* search of franchises within one industry.

Ironically, if you feel that you "don't know where to start" when choosing a franchise, you're more likely to follow the logical course of total horizontal research. If you do know where to start, it may be because you haven't fully considered the range of options available to you.

Of course, this phenomenon isn't unique to franchising. Business brokers will tell you they often advertise bars or liquor stores, because they bring the people in. People think, "Oh yeah, I'd like to run a bar"—they romanticize the concept a bit. But when they come in to talk to the broker, they usually end up buying something else. These people are also looking horizontally, and the broker plays on the appeal of the bar or liquor store to get them in the door.

It's also amazing how many knowledgeable businesspeople look at franchising horizontally rather than vertically. An experienced franchisor who was being bought out of his share of a multimillion-dollar-a-year franchise business came up to Don at a party and said, "I'm going to have some cash after this deal. Which industry in franchising do you think is hot right now?" He's in the *franchising business,* and he doesn't care which industry he gets into—he just wants to know what's hot!

Strangely, in the horizontal search, the paths of the shrewd and the emotional cross: The shrewd businessperson doesn't care about the industry he is getting into as long as she makes money; the emotional person also doesn't care about the industry she is getting into—she just wants the franchise she has "always wanted." This doesn't guarantee that either one of them is going to be successful (though shrewdness would have to be awarded the inside track). But we'd have to admit that if they both fail, one of them is going to have a heck of a lot more fun doing it than the other one!

Spotting a Growth Industry

So what's the best way to start assessing industries, to start assembling your list of possible franchises to buy into? How can you tell which field is going to experience the greatest growth in the coming years?

Do you remember *The Graduate,* that movie of the late 1960s starring Dustin Hoffman? In a famous scene in that movie, a middle-aged man at a party gives Hoffman's young, postcollegiate character some advice about a burgeoning industry: "I just want to say one word to you: *plastics.*" And that was fine advice then. Plastics *did* have a steady (if perhaps unspectacular) rise over the following two decades. (However, if that character had said "computers" to Hoffman, we'd have been much more impressed today with the prognostical abilities of the movie's writer!) The bottom line is: How do you find the "plastics" (or, indeed, the "computers") of today? How do you track the trends that lead to growth industries that can lead (ultimately) to franchising success?

It may seem like a tall order. Yet we are about to suggest not one, but *two* relatively easy ways to be on the lookout for upcoming trends:

Magazines

Have you been by one of those full-service, overflowing magazine stands lately? Not just the rack of the latest news, fashion, and gossip mags in chain bookstores or supermarkets, but the kind you find in a train station or in a college town or neighborhood, with everything from the top sellers to obscure, new, and even trade magazines. ("Trade" are those aimed at professionals in a particular field, be they doctors, travel agents, or even sanitation engineers.) If you've seen one of these magazine stands, you'll agree with us on one thing: There are too many magazines in this world! But this can be both bad and good.

It's bad for most magazine entrepreneurs, because national magazine startups cost *lots* of money (usually from $1 million just to get up, running, and out on the stands) and most of them fail.

However, this proliferation of magazines can be good for trend-watchers in two ways, because magazines are often ahead of their time. At a million bucks a throw, even the eventual failures have been *usually* well planned, with substantial market and audience research going into each launch. So if you see two or three new magazines coming out that are devoted, for example, to at-home microfarming, you know that—even if all of them eventually go under—there is *some* sort of growing buzz for at-home microfarming.

Eventually, if the trend *does* come to fruition, some magazine on the subject will usually succeed, which leads to another benefit of magazine watching. When a magazine of this sort catches on, not only does it become successful unto itself, but it often becomes a "mouthpiece" and/or clearinghouse of information for the industry, trend, or movement that helped launch it. In other words, which comes first, the chicken or the egg? Well, in this case, they both develop at the same time, and then feed off of each other's growing head of steam. The result is a prime example of that recent catchword, *synergy*.

So how do you keep on top of the world of magazines even *before* those new titles hit the newsstands? The best way we've discovered is to read *FOLIO,* which is the trade magazine for the magazine industry (there *are* magazines for just about everything!). In one easy to digest and fairly well written source, you have all the news on what's coming up and coming out in the magazine industry—and this can help clue you in to upcoming growth industries.

How valuable can this information be? We estimate that when you spot magazine-based trends early enough (and with the correct interpretation), you can gain up to a *four-year* lead-time before the trend/industry fully hits its stride and permeates the public consciousness.

Newsletters

Where do magazine entrepreneurs get *their* leading indicators? Oftentimes, the answer is through newsletters. If magazines can be (in the best cases) up to four years ahead, newsletters *can be* another four years ahead of that! But of course the farther upstream you try to track these things, the greater your chance of losing the trail. With that sort of lead time, many newsletter ideas fail or mutate beyond recognition before they are able to come to fruition. Basically, they *can* be farther ahead, but the margin for error also increases.

Our unofficial, unscientific estimate is that after four or five newsletters happen, a magazine happens. The reason? Newsletters are easier to get into, they cost less, and they can be done quickly. Instead of $1 million for a magazine, all you need for a newsletter is a word processor, a mailing list, and a postage meter!

And, much as with *FOLIO* in the magazine business, the way to track new and emerging trends in newsletters is through two publications/organizations, *The Newsletter on Newsletters,* published by the Newsletter Clearinghouse of Rhinebeck, New York (this organization also produces the *Newsletter Yearbook Directory,* an annual listing of newsletters by category and title), and the Newsletter Association of America's newsletter, based in Washington, D.C. These publications can provide you with valuable information to spot and follow new trends and industries as mirrored by emerging newsletters.

Once you have an idea of some of the industries that are hot, you can turn to other sources of research to begin fine-tuning your list. Government statistics, industry projections (especially if there is a trade association for the industry you're looking at), and even general newspaper and magazine articles are all good sources of research. (We'll suggest returning to these and similar sources later, for further research.)

Establishing the Candidates

When you reach this point in your search, you should have a good idea of your general objectives, where you stand on the risk continuum, whether you have an emotional attachment toward any particular industry or individual franchise, and, with the assistance of some savvy research, which industries seem the most promising. The next step is to identify which specific industry (or industries) and/or franchise (or franchises) you are going to pursue.

Basically, you are now going to shift your focus from broad industry trends to individual industries or businesses you might like to work in. And if you've had your heart set on a particular franchise all along, you should have a bit more of an objective idea on how its industry stacks up.

The Resources

To assist you in assembling a list of industries and franchises to consider, there are two important resources that we suggest you employ.

Franchise Source Guides

The best place to begin your list is through a book listing the majority of franchises available in all categories. One of the best books of this type is *The Sourcebook of Franchise Opportunities* by Bond & Bond. Other sources—not as detailed in their information—include the *Franchise Opportunities Handbook,* produced annually by the International Franchise Association (IFA) of Washington, D.C., and several magazinelike handbooks available at many bookstores and newsstands. See Appendix VI at the end of this book for a list of guides and how to get them.

The listings in these books typically include the name, address, and phone number of the franchisor; when the company was founded and/or started franchising; how many franchises and company-owned outlets the franchisor has (and perhaps how many states these outlets are in); the franchise fee and a range of capital requirements; and perhaps the two most important facts to consider when actually assembling your list: whether the company is actively seeking franchisees and, if so, in what areas of the country they are seeking them.

Those last two may seem like obvious points, but they can prevent you from wasting time considering options that really aren't open to you. Some established franchisors are granting new franchises only to their current franchisees; others may not be seeking franchisees in areas where you currently live or would be willing to relocate to—meaning this information should be a vital part of your screening process.

Franchise Trade Shows

Another way to gather (or refine) list-building information is to visit franchise trade shows, particularly those sponsored by the IFA. These shows are held frequently, at hotels, exposition centers, and other convention facilities.

For a nominal fee (around $3 to $5, to cover a portion of the operating expenses), the public can browse thirty to seventy booths of exhibiting franchisors. The method of presentation varies from franchisor to franchisor—some use videos, others have teams of salespeople—but the basic concept remains that they are attempting to both impress you with their franchise *and* qualify you somewhat as a potential franchisee (i.e., determine if you are serious about getting into their business, whether you can afford it, or if you are just browsing).

If they feel you are qualified, they will endeavor to take your name and address and perhaps give you a franchise brochure. Aggressive franchisors will follow up later with a phone call. (Many franchisors take your address rather than handing out the brochures directly since these brochures are usually expensive to produce and it is not cost-effective to just pass out piles of these to prospects who may not be genuinely interested.)

We strongly suggest that you do attend at least one trade show (especially one sponsored by the IFA), but we must add a few caveats to this recommendation:

1. Do your general book research before you attend a trade show.
2. Call the IFA for a list of franchisors attending the show

you will be going to—and then check them in whichever
book you have, so you are familiar with their background.
3. Bring the book with you, so you can be immediately
acquainted with important facts about any particular
franchisor (such as its age, its franchise fee, the areas in
which it is seeking franchises, etc.) before you talk to its
representatives. You'll get more out of a trade show if you
know who is going to be there, what their requirements
are, and who you might be interested in talking to *before*
you actually talk to them.

What Franchise Brochures Are and How to Get Them

Franchise brochures are the basic initial information and sales
vehicles used to promote franchises to prospective franchisees. In
the best of cases they are creatively produced, written in laymen's
terms (easy on the jargon, so as not to confuse the prospect), full
of upbeat statistics, and usually illustrated with color photography,
graphics, and perhaps charts.

The brochure's mission is to educate you on three things (in
ascending order of importance): (1) franchising in general; (2) the
market for the franchise's particular industry; and (3) the
individual franchise itself. While franchise brochures are *usually*
informative pieces, they are also infused with a decent helping of
"sizzle" (as in the classic advertising adage, "Sell the sizzle, not
the steak").

Once you have created your list, call or write the franchisor's
offices, requesting information about their franchising programs.
Or, as noted above, you can leave your name and address with a
franchisor at a trade show. Either way, you should hear from the
franchisor quickly. Franchise brochures are an important early
step in the selling process, and franchisors are not likely to delay
getting their material to an eager audience. If they *do* take an
inordinately long time to respond to your request, either they're

swamped with requests, big enough not to care about interested prospects or sales candidates, or just plain inept. Realize this and govern yourself accordingly.

How to Read a Franchise Brochure

They say you can't judge a book by its cover, and that's usually true. Even if you receive a franchise brochure that's only somewhat attractive, read it with an open mind. Many young franchisors have more to offer in the way of potential than in money to spend on a brochure. However, if the brochure's design, writing, or overall quality is noticeably substandard, so might be the franchisor.

In most cases, brochures will contain many (if not all) of the following features.

A Snappy Cover Blurb and Introduction

Franchise brochures are like any other sales/advertising vehicle—they want to grab your attention early and motivate you to read on. To that end, they usually start out with a bang on the cover and in the intro, often establishing a "clever" theme that will carry through the entire piece (e.g., using Hollywood terms—*four-star, box office success, strong supporting cast*—to describe a video-rental franchise; sporting terms for a sports memorabilia franchise, etc.).

Explanation of the Concept

This section is the meat of the brochure, telling you about the franchise's general business concept, its point(s) of difference over its competitors (both franchised and nonfranchised), how its operating system works, and the special requirements, if any, needed to run the franchise, such as previous experience in the particular industry or various professional qualifications. Also in this section, statistics supporting franchising in general will likely be presented, as may quotes or case histories of successful franchisees.

Analysis of the Market/Industry and the Franchise's Niche Therein

We're not trying to sound cynical, but you can probably guess that this section will tell you that the widget industry, for example, is booming. Which is not to say that this unfailing cheerleading is a necessarily bad thing. If you're going to put your future on the line with an XYZ Widget franchise, it's reassuring to know that there *is* a future. The best-written and -produced brochures include useful footnoted quotes on industry or franchisor statistics and trends. You can learn more by following up on these quotes and tracking down the magazine or newspaper articles quoted. This, however, is only the case in the best examples—franchise brochures usually use more loosely attributed quotes and facts (e.g., "*Newsweek* says this industry is booming!").

Background of the Company and/or Its Principal Personnel

This usually interesting section will provide historical background on the company, if there is any, and/or a capsule biography of the founder(s) or other principal personnel (if it is pertinent *and* if they are still with the company). Basically, whichever story is more cogent and/or compelling will get the biggest play. If the company is fairly new, for example, but its founder is well known in her or his field, the coverage will focus more on the founder than on the company.

List and Explanation of the Franchise's Advantages

This section tells you what you can expect to get from this franchise if you sign on as a franchisee. A known name, full training, a proven system (perhaps including proprietary computer software or various equipment), national or regional advertising, ongoing support—these are among the advantages offered by most franchisors and described in detail in this section of the brochure. Also, for those not necessarily "converted" to franchising yet, the general benefits of it as a business system are usually also summarized here.

Conclusion and Call to Action

The brochure usually wraps up with a conclusion that briefly reviews the franchise's concept and benefits and then challenges the reader to take the next step in the process—filling out the brief "evaluation form" (sort of a preapplication) often included with the brochure or by calling the franchisor's sales department.

Bearing all this in mind, sometimes what *isn't* included in a brochure can tell you as much as what is included.

Where's the Beef?

Since all franchise brochures aim to project a positive, feel-good image of the franchises they describe, it can be difficult to get a well-rounded picture of a franchise simply by reading a brochure. As you would expect, the franchise brochure is *not* going to address negatives—be they the franchisor's shaky image, the uncertain state of the industry, or the franchisor's plummeting market share. But by carefully reading a brochure and noting what *isn't* included in it, you can often discover which areas you need to investigate more deeply if you are to pursue this particular franchisor.

An example: You're reading the brochure of a long-time (but not superstar-level) franchisor. You notice that it includes neither company history nor founder/principal personnel profiles. Perhaps modesty has prevailed at this franchisor. More likely, it has undergone a management shakeup, a semirecent change of direction, or some other change that makes its history moot. This need not be a bad thing (perhaps the old direction was failing), but it *is* something you should be aware of and something you should investigate.

Similarly, if you find a brochure to be lacking in solid facts about the franchisor's field (and its place in that field), its business system, or its advantages to franchisees, you have to ask yourself: What are they leaving out and why? There's probably a reason this material has been omitted—and it's probably not a flattering one. Again, follow up with your own research. You may find your doubts erased or find that this franchisor needs to *be* erased—from your list!

Further Evaluating the Candidates

Okay. You've read your brochures, probably crossed a few more candidates off your list, and you're almost ready for the next step (and the next chapter): beginning the actual buying process by visiting franchisors. But since this can be an expensive proposition (relatively speaking, it isn't expensive when compared to what you will be investing in your eventual franchise), you want to make sure you have cut out any deadwood before you start. There's a little more research to do.

First, take a closer, long-term look at the industry (or industries) your "possibles" are in. Are they up, down, stable? What do the forecasters say about the future? And try to find out *why* things are up, down, or static. Could it be temporary? Caused by internal or external forces? How will the industry fare the next time the economy changes?

Next, do more research on the individual franchises you are considering. Are they selling more or fewer franchises than they have in the past? If the answer is more, is this true growth or just a temporary upswing? Ask the same question about gross sales at the franchised units? Are they growing? Why? Simply because of a recent price increase or due to actual, steady growth?

We suggest that you also read up on general trend analysis— the Naisbitt *Megatrends* books are good places to begin. How will the new directions charted in those books (or other future-oriented sources) affect the industries and franchises you are considering? Which franchises will benefit from likely coming trends? Which will be harmed by them—perhaps even be made obsolete? Are the target customer groups of a particular franchise a growing or shrinking demographic? Does its prime customer base cut across socioeconomic lines? Will there be more or fewer people that desire or need its service in the coming years?

The bottom line is this: The world (and the people and businesses in it) constantly undergoes change—sometimes quickly, other times slowly; sometimes for the better, other times for the worse. What you have to try and perceive, as best as you are able, is how these changes may affect the business(es) you are considering getting into.

All the knowledge and research you accumulate will help you when the time comes to make your ultimate decision. But before you do, we're going to share a little more of our accumulated knowledge with you and advise you on some characteristics of franchises that you should avoid. Think of it as the final fine-tuning of your list before you make the great leap of actually visiting franchisors and evaluating these franchises as purely financial investments.

Franchises to Avoid

In Chapter 1, we covered several general types of businesses that were not good candidates for franchising. Here, we are going to list some warning signs to look for that may indicate that an existing franchise may not be a particularly good choice. Our advice is generally to avoid the following.

Franchisors with a Single Fad Product
Remember the "glue factory" list from Chapter 1? Some of the entries are this type. Fresh muffins may be a great hit for six months or a year, but how many muffins can the public eat before they get tired of them? And how long will it be before the cookie shop next door adds them as a sideline?

Labor-intensive or Widely Unautomated Franchises

If you have followed business and societal trends for the last few years, you know how difficult it has become to attract minimum-wage workers (or even, in some areas, $5- and $6-an-hour workers). As the pool of these workers continues to dwindle and the competition for them among employers increases, many franchisees are going to find their labor costs increasing dramatically. Instead of being saddled with a franchise that relies too heavily on this uncertain pool of workers, you want a franchise operating system that minimizes your overhead costs and, at the same time, minimizes the potential for human error. If the business you like intrinsically requires a staff, look for a franchise system that keeps that staff as small as possible, which could be the franchise's competitive edge.

But even a business that you can run as a one-person shop needs proven systems in place, be they mechanical, computerized, or otherwise efficient. Because if it's all up to *you* and *your* skills, why in the world would you be paying the franchisor to *allow* you to do this? Remember: You are *buying* a franchise, and, logically, you have every right to expect the franchisor to provide you with value for your money—in this case, the value of an established, effective, and efficient business system.

Franchisors with Legal Problems or a Multitude of Failed Franchisees

Have you uncovered stories of legal travails in the background of a particular franchisor? Has it recently lost a significant number of franchisees? As you can well imagine, these are not good signs. If these problems were in the fairly distant past, perhaps the franchisor has turned things around. If the problems are more recent, watch out—you may be about to step into a viper's nest of hassles. Although the franchisor has to fully disclose this sort of information in later stages of discussion, you are better off knowing it now—all the more reason to do thorough research.

Franchisors Whose Unit Sales Have Been Declining or Are Below Industry Averages

Is the bloom off the rose? Did this franchisor once rule its market but has slipped in the face of growing competition? If so, maybe you should be looking at one of those competitors instead. Also, are its sales—even if they *are* growing—below the average for its industry? If everyone else is making more money in this field, what is this franchisor doing wrong? Remember, for your best shot at success, you don't want a business whose performance is average, or even good—you want *superior*. It's like the old story about the experienced jockey who is asked the best way to win the Kentucky Derby. "Ride the fastest horse," he simply replied. You don't want just any old nag—you want the fastest horse!

Franchisors with Limited Ongoing Support or Advertising

Again, what are you paying for? A percentage of your sales will be going to royalties, and you have a right to expect service and support for your money. Franchisors who provide little more than a trademark and a kind word should definitely be avoided.

Are You Ready for a Deeper Commitment?

If you've followed our lead and fully examined the wide world of possibilities that exist within franchising, you should be excellently prepared to make your ultimate decision. We know it's not a quick and easy path, but we think you'll agree that in the long run it's more than worth it. Congratulations!

After you've completed the various steps covered in this chapter, you should have any number of qualified, screened, and fully researched franchisors remaining on your list. If your list is still large when you reach this point, it doesn't necessarily mean you did anything wrong—perhaps you could be happy and successful with any of them. You will begin to find out soon. If there's only one franchisor left, perhaps that's *the* one for you—but don't be blind to other possibilities that you may not have considered. And if you end up eliminating all of the franchisors from your list, don't be discouraged. Maybe you just started on the wrong track. After doing all of that work, you will know more about franchising and the various fields it embraces, and you can start a more focused and, presumably, a more successful search.

For those of you who *definitely* had a favorite in mind before you even started researching, it will be interesting to see how your favorite did. If you faithfully do all of the research we suggest and season your emotion with some logic, you'll be in a much better spot than when you wanted a particular franchise solely because you liked its product.

Now comes the next step in the process of becoming a franchisee—one that requires a deeper commitment in terms of time and money. You're going to visit one or more franchisors, see their headquarters, meet their executives, and tour their operating units. You are also going to examine disclosure documents and earnings claims, contact current (and perhaps former) franchisees, and generally learn more about franchising and your ambitions within it. Perhaps most importantly in the long run, you are going to closely examine franchising as an investment in terms of your time *and* money.

In the next chapter, we will take you from the point of having a finely honed, researched list to its logical conclusion—through the buying process and the closing.

In other words, if you have come this far, the next chapter will help take you the final steps to your destination: becoming a franchisee and business owner.

Chapter Five

Becoming a
Franchisee, Part III:
The Final Steps

You probably know the old saw about having children: It's hard to *be* a parent—but it's easy to *become* one!

On the other hand, becoming a franchisee isn't nearly as easy as becoming a parent, and being one usually isn't as hard. But like parenthood, being a franchisee can be a very rewarding adventure.

At this point, you have come far in your quest to become a franchisee, but there is still a considerable distance to go—the distance that separates someone who is *interested* in becoming a franchisee and someone who *is* a franchisee.

In this chapter, we will take you through the final steps between where you are now and where you could be. We will cover visiting a franchisor's headquarters, getting and examining the necessary documentation, investigating sources of financing, and perhaps most importantly—often least understood— becoming a franchisee purely as an investment.

But, before we fully explore and explain the final steps you must take to become a franchisee, we'll present a realistic look at some reasons why even sound-seeming franchised outlets can fail.

Why Franchises Fail

As you should realize by now, franchising isn't a "sure thing." The U.S. Department of Commerce estimates an annual failure rate for franchised businesses much lower than the failure rate for new, independent businesses (estimated by various sources as ranging from 30 to 90 percent during the first five years of operation). But that fact will be of little comfort to you if you find yourself among the small minority who *do* fail.

The fact of the matter is, despite the proven record of franchising, some franchises *do* fail—and some of these are even franchises of well established, "superstar" franchisors. The precise reasons for franchise failures can be as many as the number of failed outlets itself, but some are more common than others. Here are eleven common reasons why franchises fail.

Poor Business Concept or System

If a franchise's basic concept or operating system is fundamentally flawed, no amount of hard work on the part of a franchisee will likely overcome this handicap. It is therefore vitally important to fully research a franchise's history and current status before you buy. If it's a longtime franchisor, has it had a rash of recent franchisee failures? If it's a new franchisor or it's expanding into a new area, conduct an informal survey of friends and associates. Ask them if they need or desire the product or service the franchise is offering. No matter the "good deal" you can get by becoming (for example) the first franchisee of the Acme Pet Psychiatrist chain, it isn't going to be worth your time and money if not enough people want to purchase your services. The same can be true of businesses that are not proven, such as a business tied too heavily to a fad that eventually fades.

Poor Location

The old quip about "location, location, location" being the three most important considerations in determining a retailer's success is at least partly true. While a good or "perfect" location cannot assure a franchise of success, a bad location can doom even the most promising of franchises. What's a bad location? It can range from being located in a run-down or otherwise dangerous neighborhood to being in a brand-new shopping mall away from established traffic patterns. Fast food franchises can usually survive in either strictly residential or business areas (although in areas with different peak times of traffic, they may have different peak hours and even different operating hours). Housewares or business-equipment franchises, on the other hand, would likely do best in an area close to their respective target customers. If a particular franchisor has shown success in helping franchisees find and secure locations, this can be very valuable assistance, even if there is an additional charge for it.

Weak Management

In most cases, franchisees need to be actively involved in the day-to-day operation of their franchises. This is a major reason most franchisors will not sell franchises to "absentee investors," who buy the unit but do not actively participate in running it. For example, we would conservatively guess that there are literally *thousands* of established professionals who would love to buy a McDonald's franchise as an investment. But McDonald's won't sell to absentee investors. Their attitude is "You want a McDonald's franchise? Fine, but you'll have to quit your job and work the store." Of course, huge franchise investments such as hotels are an exception. Franchisees of these types of businesses often just provide the money; they usually hire a staff or a management company to run the business for them.

Incompatibility of Franchisee Skills with Those Needed to Successfully Run the Franchise

Or, in other words, has a franchisee sent an administrator or a manager (i.e., himself or herself) to do the job of a salesman? As we pointed out in the test in Chapter 3, the most successful franchisees have at least *some* sales ability, are people-oriented, don't mind hard work, and are eager to learn. The most meticulous franchisors look for these traits in potential franchisees—as well as other, specific characteristics that they know from experience are necessary or beneficial in their line of business. But if a franchisor doesn't care and a franchisee fools himself into believing she has what it takes, the result can be a failed franchise. If you don't like or can't do the particular work that a particular franchise requires, it's not the right franchise for you, no matter how attractive the investment.

Poor Profit Potential

Though obvious, this point needs to be stated. If a franchised business has to produce huge sales numbers from the day it opens just to cover the costs of goods and salaries *and* the royalty rate, where is your profit margin going to come from? There *are* some exceptions (such as low overhead, one- or two-person franchises, especially in the janitorial/maid field), but in general, businesses with inherently small profit margins, low sales figures, or high prices (and low volume) are usually *not* good candidates for success in franchising. You'll want to make more money on your investment than you could by simply putting your money in a bank or government bond!

Too Much Competition

This ties in with location. Although several different types of fast food restaurants on the same street can help each other by increasing customer traffic in the entire area, *too many* restaurants on the same street can hurt the entire group by diluting the customer base. How many is too many? When is local competition a threat rather than just a source of healthy rivalry? Franchisors should have some answers, backed up with research and experience, to these questions. If they don't, be careful. The strength of being part of a franchise does not guarantee success, and there have been plenty of examples of even well-known franchises faring poorly in competition against locally popular businesses in the same field. For example, Domino's Pizza experienced years of difficulty cracking the Chicago market, because that city boasts a large number of long-established pizza parlors (who also deliver); these have carved out individual niches and engendered fierce loyalties. There are also several excellent regional franchises in the Chicago area, like Pizzas by Marchelloni, which resist inroads in their market areas by national chains.

Territory Too Small

If the area from which a franchise is supposed to draw its primary customers is too small to provide an adequate base, the franchise can be endangered before it even opens. Of course, some franchise territories are limited to the site of the outlet itself, but most franchises allow a general radius in which another corporate-owned or franchised outlet *of the same chain* will be located. It can be hard enough to compete against *other* chains and local businesses, but a franchisee forced to compete with its own franchisor has an uphill battle indeed. The importance of territory size becomes even more critical when your franchise is a service-oriented one that needs to make sales calls within its assigned area.

Poor Support by the Franchisor

Training, advertising, general publicity, contracts for supplies that have been negotiated with the power of multiple buying, ongoing assistance—these are the sorts of things for which franchisees pay royalties to franchisors. We will examine royalties and other financial- and investment-related aspects of becoming a franchisee later in this chapter. But if these services are lacking, while the royalties are still being paid, a franchise will face all the disadvantages that nonaffiliated businesses face while having 4 to

10 percent *less* net revenue to show for it! Checking with a franchisor's current franchisees, as we will explain later in this chapter, can divulge whether the franchisor provides its franchisees with the proper level of support they need—and which they pay for!

Fraud on the Part of the Franchisor

Fraud occurs less frequently than it did during franchising's early, less regulated years. But, every so often, you hear or read about a franchise that has folded due to its franchisor's financial or operational vagaries. The franchisees of these failed systems either go under, attempt to operate as a renamed independent, or in rare cases are snapped up as franchisees of a competing franchise. We cover the legal aspects of franchising, including some historical examples of fraud, in Chapter 9.

Lack of Working Capital

As we saw in the results of the franchisor survey in Chapter 3, franchisors generally consider it more important for a franchisee to have at least *some* money in reserve than for a franchisee to have his or her "last dime" in the business. Sure, complete financial commitment is desirable—but it's even more important for a franchisee to be able to weather any financial storms that may appear during the first months of a franchise's operation. Lack of liquid capital to cover these sorts of emergencies has doomed many a franchisee to failure.

Unforeseen Disasters

Even though this isn't a category that you can consciously try to avoid or otherwise prepare for, it *can be* a considerable cause of franchisee failure. For example, a Dunkin' Donuts near Don's office in a Chicago suburb was basically put out of operation for about five months when the road it was on was closed for widening. Another good example of an unanticipated problem occurred in the late 1970s when McDonald's outlets in and around Atlanta were rumored to be serving burgers with worms ground into the meat (the rumor later spread throughout the country). Of course, the rumor was completely untrue—for one thing, as Ray Kroc quickly pointed out, worms cost *more* per pound than beef!—but its circulation *did* negatively affect the chain's sales throughout the Southeast for a few months until the charges had been proved unfounded and the damage somewhat controlled. It is quite possible that a more damaging rumor aimed at a weaker franchise could cause such sales fall-offs as to induce individual—or even chainwide—failures. Unforeseen occurrences can also include "acts of God," such as tornadoes, earthquakes, and hurricanes; insurance can help in these instances, but the setback can still ruin unprepared (or underprepared) franchisees. We hate to sound pessimistic, but it is always a good idea to think of the *worst* things that *could* happen to your business, and then, whenever possible, prepare for these potential calamities as best you can.

Sufficiently warned? Well, we wouldn't want you to accuse us of making franchising sound like a simple stroll down Easy Street! Seriously, however, we do believe franchising can be an excellent form of business for the right people. Bear in mind that many of the reasons for failure we enumerated also apply to nonfranchised businesses—and that your franchisor should help you anticipate and deal with most of these potential danger areas.

Now that you've fully researched your choices of potential franchisors (using the guidelines in the preceding chapter), you're ready for the next logical step—learning more about the franchisor (or franchisors) in which you are most interested.

Do's and Don'ts of Purchasing a Franchise

Do:

- Hire an attorney who is experienced in franchising.
- Contact the International Franchise Association for information on the franchise industry.

- Establish a business plan, including your personal goals including strengths and weaknesses.
- Ensure that you have adequate financial resources before committing to a business out of your financial range.
- Add an additional three to six months of working capital in addition to that recommended by the franchisor.
- Attend franchising expositions.
- Meet the president of the company before purchasing a franchise.
- Ensure that adequate training is provided initially and continually.
- Review agreement and understand what your territory is and what protection you have against future expansion.

Don't:

- Purchase a franchise without researching the background of the company and reviewing the offering circular.
- Limit yourself to a particular type of service or product.
- Make a final commitment without speaking to several franchisees, preferably at their sites.
- Underestimate the period before you break even.
- Get involved with a franchisor that does not investigate your background.
- Buy a franchise without understanding the extent of operations assistance available.
- Buy a franchise without understanding what fees are involved and what products and services you will be expected to purchase from the franchisor.

Finding Out about the Franchisor

To make the best, most informed decision regarding a franchisor that you can, you have to know as much as you can find out about the franchisor. In our view, this can be primarily divided into four parts:

1. Visiting the franchisor;
2. obtaining and analyzing documents and forms;
3. talking to current franchisees; and
4. looking at earnings claims.

Visiting the Franchisor

As we've said, it takes time and money to become a franchisee—not simply to buy a franchise, but to investigate your options. You should allot sufficient time to visit at least three franchisors. You should also spend time visiting individual franchises. Of course, this could mean spending money as well to travel.

At the franchisor's headquarters, you will likely do the following: meet the franchisor's upper-level management, see its corporate facility, receive important legal documents, be asked to fill out an application (if one hadn't been sent to you previously), and generally get to know more about the franchisor. Make no mistake about it—*you* are also going to be evaluated and, if you are acceptable to the franchisor, you are also going to be more or less continuously and subtly persuaded of the advantages of becoming a franchisee of this franchisor's system.

It's also in your best interest, if you are married, to bring your spouse along on this visit. Even if he or she isn't going to directly work in or with your franchise, buying a franchise is still a big commitment, and is worthy of consideration by both members of a life partnership. Sure, a full-blown visit—if the franchisor is located in a distant city—may cost you around $1,000 in transportation and accommodation for two, but in general, we think it's worth it. You're about to invest your life and your future in this venture (not to mention substantially more than $1,000)—so don't be penny-wise and pound-foolish. Also, your willingness to invest some initial time and money to make this visit shows the franchisor you are serious and are ready to fully commit even *more* time and money to the right franchisor. If the franchisor is savvy and is truly interested in you as a franchisee, you'll be treated with respect, not as a mere browser or "tire kicker."

That last point about being treated with respect brings up a good question: In general, how should you expect to be treated when visiting a franchisor? Our answer to that is that you should be treated professionally and as if your time is valuable. Beyond this answer, we have some twofold advice:

1. Yes, *you* are also being evaluated by the franchisor, but that doesn't mean they have the right to treat you like some sort of freshman fraternity pledge. If you are not happy with the levels of attention, information, or cooperation that you are getting from a particular franchisor, it is not likely a good match for you (or, perhaps, for anybody).

2. The other side of this coin is you shouldn't become overly impressed by the attention that is likely to be lavished on you by the franchisor's staff. This is, after all, their job. Yes, you should be treated well, but you shouldn't allow such treatment to blind you to your real mission—finding out as much as possible about the franchisor and its franchises. (And, as we have noted, inappropriate levels of fawning and attention *may* indicate an unhealthy eagerness on the part of the franchisor to get you to commit.)

The perception among potential franchisees is often one of, "I have money, I can buy what I want." But, of course, the actual situation is that a franchisor has to want *you* as a franchisee before they'll want your money (unless, as we've said, they're unscrupulous or just don't care). You may have time, money, desire, and experience, but they still may or *may not* want you. Both parties have something to bring to the deal, so there has to be a mutually beneficial agreement. So, to bring about this possible "coming together" of interested parties, they will interview you as much as you interview them.

Documents and Forms

A big part of visiting a franchisor is obtaining the necessary documents and forms, most notably the offering circular and the franchise agreement. (The other major form is the franchisee application—sometimes euphemistically referred to as an "evaluation" or "questionnaire"; this is usually sent out to prospective franchisees ahead of time, but may be provided during the visit instead.) We examine what to look for in the offering circular and the franchise agreement in Chapter 9 which covers legal topics.

Brief definitions of these forms are as follows: The offering circular provides vital and legally required information about the franchisor and its franchising program; the franchise agreement is a contract specifying the terms under which the franchisee and franchisor will do business together. This material can be a bit daunting, but it is required, and the information it presents will help you make the most educated final decision possible.

The other major form we mentioned above is the application, which you may have received before your visit. This form usually asks for detailed personal information about work history, finances, health, education, family, and various other categories. This can be an intimidating document (depending upon its tone), but, as is the case in most important personal and business dealings, the best way to fill it out is candidly and fully. You can be certain that, unless this franchisor is bumbling and desperate for franchisees (*and* their cash!), the information you provide will be checked—so be certain that it is correct.

Talking to Current Franchisees

Hoover Vacuum Cleaners used to use a motto that still concisely points out the value of the opinion of an experienced customer: "Ask the woman who owns one." Of course, even if that customer opinion is *negative,* it can be of just as much value, if not more, to the person considering the purchase. The same sort of horse's mouth information should be an essential part of evaluating a particular franchisor. But instead of asking a franchised chain's *customers* (i.e., those who buy its burgers, computers, or shoe-shines), you need to ask the "consumers" who bought the franchise itself—you need to ascertain the opinions and experiences of a system's franchisees.

Start with information provided to you by the franchisor—a list of its franchisees, which may or may not be complete. Not every state requires that all franchisees be listed, but, even if they are not all detailed, the total *number* of franchisees must be provided. So your first bit of analysis is to determine how forthright the franchisor has been in disclosing this information. Does it provide only as many franchisees as it has to list? Or is the franchisor more frank—perhaps even listing *all* of its franchisees? If a franchisor discloses only the minimum amount of franchisees that they are required to give you, they may be trying to put a happy face on this part of their disclosure. This partial list may be only their system's best franchisees, in which case, you should do some independent research and come up with the names of a few franchisees who are *not* on the provided list. Calling these other franchisees—as well as those on the "approved" list—can help give you a more balanced picture of being a franchisee of this particular franchise company.

Using this list, make some calls to a decent-size sampling of these franchisees. If at all possible, we suggest that you obtain a sample of at least twenty-five selected at random. It's a good idea to poll franchisees in various areas of the country, perhaps with a heavier concentration on franchisees in and around the area in which you are most interested in locating your outlet. And, if such information is provided or can be obtained from current franchisees or another source, it can be additionally illuminating to talk to one or more former franchisees, especially those who have recently left the system.

What should you say to these franchisees? You should be sure to fully identify yourself, telling them that you are considering becoming an XYZ franchisee, and that you would like to ask them a few questions about their franchise and their experiences with the franchisor. Don't be surprised if some do not wish to talk or want to take down your questions and get back to you (they may want to clear you and your questions through the franchisor, or they may just be very busy running their own businesses)—but most will be used to such calls and should be happy to share information.

When you do start to ask them your questions, it's best to

begin with general, nonfinancial ones. Ask them things like: How long have you been an XYZ franchisee? Have you been satisfied with the support you received from the franchisor? What do you know now that you wish you knew when you first became a franchisee? What advice would you give someone considering becoming an XYZ franchisee? After getting answers to these sorts of questions, you can then move on to more specific inquiries. We strongly suggest you take written notes during this process—we've found that a short pencil is better than a long memory.

You may want to preface your financial questions by telling the franchisee something to the effect that you realize financial information can be both a speculative and very personal thing, but you would appreciate getting their input on purchasing an XYZ as a purely financial endeavor. Try to make these questions broad and nonpersonal—such as, "In your experience, what sort of annual rate of return on investment can an XYZ franchisee expect in their first few years in operation?" rather than, "How much money did you make in your first few years?"

Other questions to ask can include: How much money should an XYZ franchisee plan to have to pay for the total franchise investment? How much should an XYZ franchisee pay either himself or an employee to do the franchise's "main" job (whether that job is sales, supervision, or burger-flipping)? What amount of money would you counsel an XYZ franchisee to have in reserve for "unexpected" expenses in the first year or two? And, finally, you may be able to ask and get an answer to the $64,000 question: How much did your franchise gross last year?

To be sure, some franchisees may not want to tell you everything you want to know about these perhaps sensitive subjects. And even if they do answer all of your questions completely, you shouldn't place 100 percent reliance on the responses. After all, as far as these franchisees know, you could be someone from their franchisor checking up on them, a spy for a competitor trying to gain an advantage, or even an IRS agent calling them! These are all good reasons that, even though you should make these sorts of calls, you shouldn't have to count them as your only source of information. All the more reason that more franchisors should provide potential franchisees with complete, candid, and clear earnings claims (covered below).

Looking at Earnings Claims

First of all, we'd like to say that there *are* laws pertaining to the disclosure of potential earnings or revenues, but you shouldn't believe any franchisor who tells you it's "against the law" or that he's "not allowed" to disclose such information. What *is* true is that it's against the law to disclose information on financial performance in any other way than that prescribed by the government. And, of course, franchisors are not *required* to disclose this financial information. Our research indicates that some 80 percent do *not* do so. A growing number of franchisors, however, seem to be doing it more regularly, and we think even more should consider doing it. We believe that full disclosure of earnings can only help both sides understand the entire situation more clearly. (We include more information about earnings claims—from both the franchisor and franchisee sides—in Chapter 9.)

In our view, it is unfortunate that the majority of franchisors do *not* provide these documents, which can be enlightening, informative, and useful (both to the franchisee and the franchisor—nothing can help to sell franchises faster than being able to show they can make money!). Even when franchisors *do* provide earnings claims, they are often skewed by a desire to be precisely safe or to err on the side of conservatism. Some claims show only the performances of company-owned units or an "average" of all outlets in the system.

Some franchisors use earnings claims not to inform but to reduce their risk of a lawsuit by showing only stores that *aren't* doing well. One major food franchisor used to issue an earnings claim that showed that *every store* that opened managed to *lose* $200,000. Now, you know that isn't true—the company would have folded up their tents long ago if 100 percent of their franchisees were losing money. The reason for these very pessimistic figures was that if someone bought a franchise and *did* lose money, they wouldn't be able to come after the franchisor saying that they had been misled about the financial risks. The franchisor could respond that the franchisee had been told up front that they would lose $200,000! A funny story, yes, but this example borders on abuse of what can (and should) be a valuable tool for both sides.

If a franchisor has elected not to prepare and present an earnings claim, should that make you suspicious? No—remember that four out of five franchisors *don't*. It just means you'll have to rely more heavily on your own research and estimates of the potential of the business. When provided, however, the information in an earnings claim can help in the next stage of your overall evaluation of a franchisor (or franchisors)—looking at franchising as an investment.

What you *should* be suspicious about is if a franchisor gives you figures that aren't in the offering circular. For instance, a salesman might casually drop a remark to the effect that the last franchise he sold did $20,000 in sales just last week, but if it isn't in the legal documents, don't rely on it! And wonder to yourself, "Is he trying to put something over on me?"

After the Research

You've done plenty of research at this point, including visiting the franchisor, and you've been given the necessary documents. Perhaps you have even been told or will be told shortly that you are acceptable as a franchisee candidate. That's great! But, as we note more fully in Chapter 9, there is a required ten-business-day waiting period after receiving the offering circular during which no money can change hands. And during this period, you need to make another analysis (perhaps an even larger one than any of the others you have made) of the franchise you are considering buying. Before you commit to purchasing a particular franchise, you need to examine the transaction in terms of its impact as an investment.

Franchising As an Investment

Something we have observed over and over again in franchising is that too many people look at becoming a franchisee as simply "buying a job." In our opinion, not nearly enough potential franchisees look at it as an *investment,* too. Of course, buying a franchise *is* an investment, of both time and money, and, as with other investments, you should evaluate franchises based on the estimated return you can expect to get out of it.

Therefore, for those of you who are more financially oriented—or perhaps even more importantly, for those of you who are *not* financially savvy but who know that you should be or who would like to be—here is a methodology of how prospective franchisees should look at this portion of the franchising equation. (Those of you who are totally unfamiliar with financial and cash-flow analysis would do well to read Joe's *How to Write a Winning Business Plan* [Simon & Schuster, 1988], paying special attention to the material on pro formas.)

Becoming Educated Regarding Franchise Investments

Among the higher-priced investment franchises (such as hotels/motels, etc.), the buyers are, more often than not, "high roller" types with financial advisors who help them closely examine the purely investment side of becoming a franchisee. But in the lower price range (say $50,000 to $250,000), there is often a lack of knowledge and/or a lack of professional advisory services, which is why we're going to look at franchising now in strictly financial terms. We're going to treat your money as your slave, and put it to work for you.

The important yet simple point to consider is you should get as favorable and as competitive a rate of return as you possibly can for your franchise investment. But what should this rate be? Where do you find out what a reasonable rate of return is for your dollar? The first step is to look at what you can expect to make from comparable investments. For example, as this is being written, if you invest money in a ten-year Treasury note, you can expect to earn approximately 6 percent annually on your money; that 6 percent can be referred to as "the risk-free rate of return." If you take no risk with your money, you can earn 6 percent on it by doing nothing other than tying it up for a certain amount of time. Presumably, looking at it logically, you should therefore be able to earn something in excess of 6 percent by being willing to take more risk. Of course, there is no *guarantee* on the success of businesses, even franchised ones, and that's why we say you're taking a risk.

Evaluating the Risk of a Franchise Investment

A principal tenet of investing says "The higher the risk, the higher the return you should expect." Going back to the risk continuum we showed you in Chapter 4, the logical interpretation is that the greater the risk you're willing to take (by buying a newer franchise or a franchise in an unproven market), the greater the hoped-for return from that franchise should be. And, in general, how can you measure the risk of a franchising investment? The age and size of a franchisor is a good place to start. Usually, if a franchise system has been around for awhile and has multiple units, it has proven itself in a variety of markets—and *some* degree of risk has been taken out.

Another measure of risk is the answers to these two questions: (1) How many units has the franchisor sold recently? and (2) How many of the franchisor's franchisees have failed recently? Franchisors are required to list, in the disclosure documents they furnish potential franchisees, a list of (1) people who own a franchise (often including the date the franchises were sold or opened); and (2) the number of franchisees that have been terminated or have gone out of business in the last three years. This information will help you answer the aforementioned questions.

First of all, has the franchisor sold many recent units? Unless it is a brand-new franchisor, you should expect to see *some* recent sales. If there aren't very many sales, is it because the franchisor is very discriminating when it comes to selecting franchisees? Or is it because, perhaps, that potential franchisees have found the *franchisor* to be undesirable?

Next, check the number, and more importantly, the *percentage* of a franchisor's failed franchisees. Using the generally accepted 5-percent-per-year closure rate of franchises as a general rule of thumb, determine if the franchisor's failure rate is higher or lower. If 10, 15, or even 20 percent of their franchisees have gone out of business in any recent year, something is wrong with that franchisor—whether it has five or five thousand franchises. Also, what are the percentages by year the last few years? Is the proportion of failures falling or rising? (If it's falling, perhaps the franchisor's "bad times" are ending and it *is* a good time to buy.)

The bottom line is that if the total number of failed franchisees exceeds 5 percent of a franchisor's total outlets, it means this franchisor has a higher failure rate than most other franchisors. This could be due to poor selection of franchisees, bad locations, incomplete training programs, tough competition, flawed expansion strategies, or incompetent management on the franchisor level. Or maybe the franchised business in question is a lemon! Whatever the reasons, you need to weigh the factors before you buy.

When you purchase stock, you or your professional advisors look at its earnings and past performance—and it should be no different when it comes to buying a franchise. Looking at the comparative failure rate of a franchisor's franchisees can be one of the greatest single factors in determining overall risk.

More Risk Equals More (Expected) Return

When trying to look more precisely at risk, particularly at the higher end of the risk scale, things aren't quite as clear-cut as stated above. For example, you might find a franchise system that has higher-than-average failure rates, but whose general concept and business system you judge to be very solid. This might be a good, worthwhile risk, you deduce. You could then perhaps seek to buy out an established but struggling franchisee of this franchise, perhaps at much less than it would cost to buy a new outlet. And, *if* the only reasons the previous franchisee failed is that he or she lacked good individual management skills or wasn't using the right approach for his or her individual market, you might be able to make a much more successful go at it—and realize a hefty return on your investment in the process. But of course there *is* risk involved. What if the reason the franchise was failing was the basic concept and system *weren't* as solid as you thought? That's where the risk lies—in determining if a franchise in general or a specific unit is going to be successful. And the higher the risk, the higher estimated return you should expect to achieve before you decide to buy.

How Much Are You Worth to Yourself As an Employee?

Before you can determine your potential return on an investment in a franchise, you must consider an important concept that you may have overlooked or may not have properly assessed. Namely, you should be fairly compensated for the time you spend acting as a manager or "employee" of your franchised business on a day-to-day basis. However, before you start figuring just how generous you're going to be to yourself, you have to realize that the salary you should receive should only be *whatever the fair rate is for the job you're going to do* (such as managing a restaurant or changing a car's oil or whatever).

It doesn't matter that you might have been a top-flight salesman or a CEO making six figures before you became a franchisee. You're a lube jockey or a fry cook now (in addition, of course, to being a franchisee and business owner). Your CEO or sales skills are not needed in that position, so you shouldn't expect to make what you made before—not as a *salary,* anyway. As an investment, you may well eventually make far more than you made before. And what should be a fair rate to pay yourself? The amount you would pay someone else to do the same job! Otherwise you're overpaying the employee (yourself) and under-estimating the return to the investor (yourself).

Only after a fair salary for a manager is awarded to the owner (or whoever is going to do that job) can you calculate profit, and then return on investment.

Estimating Return

As we have said, there is more risk in investing in a franchise than in (for example) Treasury notes. And, on this higher risk end of the spectrum, you need to look for higher rates of return to make things worth your time and investment. But how high is higher?

Generally, you should look for at least one and a half to two times the risk-free rate of return on capital for most sorts of franchise investments. That is to say that if you could get 8 percent risk-free (as we noted above), you should expect to get 12 percent to 16 percent, depending upon the risk involved (i.e., 16 percent for the riskiest, down to around 12 percent for less risky—but still not "blue chip"—franchises). And how much can you expect to make on a blue chip franchise, such as a McDonald's? About the middle of the range is a good expectation—the average return is about 13 to 14 percent. (Tales of McDonald's franchisees making 20 or 25 percent on what is a relatively riskless proposition are definitely not unheard of, but don't weep in envy over these high figures. Either pony up the dough and get in the long line for a McDonald's franchise, or better yet, try and discover the *next* McDonald's, and get in on its ground floor.) All of these figures are standards to give you an idea of what to expect; as with any venture involving some amount of risk, the actual percentages may vary within these ranges. Or, of course, they may *never* materialize.

Remember that newer franchises may not have rosy histories of earnings or large numbers of outlets. But keep the general history of franchising in mind as you ponder these low (or nonexistent) numbers—for example, hamburger stands, video stores, and fast lube places all struggled at first until they became accepted and are now in general very successful and widespread franchised business. So if the concept seems strong and poised to succeed, you might wish to ignore anemic numbers, but you should expect to be compensated for this faith with a higher potential return on your investment.

Professional venture capital investment firms—of which there are several hundred in the United States—look to be compensated even *higher* than typical franchise rates when they make a decision to invest in a company. These professional financial risk takers regularly look for a return on investment from 35 percent to 70 percent annually—even up to *90 percent*. If you want a shot at these sorts of rates of return, we suggest you look at different business arenas than franchising. Instead, start your own business. Establish a copy of the video store or fast-food outlet that you think is a winner, and if you're successful, *all* of the returns are yours. But keep in mind the high failure rate for independent businesses most sources report. Yes, you *may* make more, but you're risking *much* more.

Comparing Initial Fees and Royalty Amounts

Two figures are important to understand when fully analyzing the financial end of owning a franchise: the amount of the initial franchise fee and the percentage of the ongoing royalty, both of which are paid to the franchisor. Below we will look at significant points and possible misunderstandings pertaining to each of these.

Franchise Fees

The general rule of thumb for initial fees is: The greater the amount of the total initial investment, the lower the franchise fee should be as a percentage of the investment. This rule, such as it is, pertains only to single units, rather than multiunit, area development, or subfranchise arrangements. The reason is franchisors don't want to create an impediment (through the imposition of gouging financial requirements) to people wanting to get into their business. For example, McDonald's charges a $22,500 franchise fee—and you might think, "They could charge whatever amount they want—even more than *ten times* that figure—and people would still line up to become a McDonald's franchisee." But McDonald's would rather see their franchisees have plenty of money in reserve to run the business or to maybe even open another outlet.

The flip side of this equation is that in service-type franchises (such as cleaning services or professional consultants), the fee may be half or more of the total investment. The reason? These are generally *not* capital-intensive businesses—franchisees usually don't have to buy land or buildings or extensive in-plant equipment—and therefore the fee is much higher in comparison to the other costs. Does this mean that these fees are high simply because that's what the franchisor feels it can charge? Usually not, because in these cases what you're paying for—at usually a fraction of a price it would cost to develop them yourself—are the systems, technology, and materials the franchisor has developed, plus, if appropriate, the advantages of cooperative buying and advertising.

In short, you should try to determine if the initial fee seems fair, but you should not put overriding importance on this figure. By itself, neither the franchise fee nor the royalty percentage (covered below) should be a factor influencing whether or not someone becomes a franchisee of a particular franchisor. Instead, you must look at the entire investment and what you can expect in return.

Prospective franchisees need to get over the barrier they often have in their minds that they're paying a fee of, say, $50,000 just to "join the club"—a sort of initiation fee. Franchisees are *not* joining a club or simply paying for the rights to a business's name (at least, they *shouldn't* be merely paying for a name—we've shown earlier all the components that a franchisee should expect in return for their investment).

You should also realize the franchise fee is the only source of initial income to the franchisor while they train you and set you up. You *may* be paying $500,000 for your franchise (excluding the fee), but you have to remember that amount doesn't go to the franchisor. Instead it purchases land, a building, equipment, inventory, and so forth.

The Ongoing Royalty Percentage

If, as we've shown you, franchisees are not paying a capricious initiation fee to franchisors, neither are they paying a permanent percentage of their income to the franchisor just for being allowed to operate. Again, that royalty pays for support, advice, research and development, and, above all else, a proven business system and the expertise to successfully operate it. Look at the situation this way: Would you rather pay nothing to no one but have a much higher chance of losing your investment? Or would you be willing to pay perhaps 8 percent in royalties for an established concept and earn maybe 15 to 20 percent on your capital?

Once the general overall benefits of the royalty have been determined, next you have to look at the specific figure and what you can expect to get for it. It is important not to judge a royalty simply by its gross amount—that is, don't look at the situation as follows: The XYZ Company charges 8 percent, but the ABC Company only charges 6 percent. You have to examine it in terms of what it will cost you in real dollars and what it gets you as an investor. In other words, 8 percent *of what* and *for what,* compared to 6 percent *of what* and *for what?* What are the franchise's sales likely to be? What services will the amount buy you?

For example, in the case of McDonald's, between royalty and rent (because they typically own the land on which their franchises are located), they charge their franchisees approximately 12 percent of total gross sales, but the annual return on investment these franchises realize can be from 13 and up! On the other hand, if John's Burgers charges only a 4 percent royalty and returns maybe 8 percent on your investment, you're not being logical if you go with John's only because 4 is less than 16. (Obviously, this oversimplifies things a bit, but you get the point.) Don't get lulled into thinking that low royalty amounts will save you money. Low royalties generally translate into a low level of service and a low return. Of course, if all other things are equal (such as total investment, national or regional reputation, level of service, and rate of return), but a certain franchisor's rate is lower, you should probably go with the lower rate.

You have to expect that the franchisor should realize a financial return for establishing you in business and for providing you with their proven expertise (that "safety net" we discussed earlier in the book). And, as we've shown, the initial fee sure doesn't cover those things with much of a profit margin. So don't look at a royalty as a negative and don't begrudge the franchisor that money—it is merely part of the cost of doing business as a franchisee.

Now that you've got a better idea of what franchising can do for your money, how do you get the money to accomplish all of this?

Financing Options

Of course, you've likely been thinking about this all along. How am I going to pay for this? We're going to touch on only a *few* points here—entire books have been written about financing franchises or other small businesses. (For additional information, we recommend the financing section of Joe's *How to Start, Finance, and Manage Your Own Small Business,* which we referred to in Chapter 3.)

In general, since methods of financing can vary greatly from person to person and from situation to situation, we can only offer some advice, some facts, and a little direction. The first and perhaps most important rule of financing a franchise is not to underestimate the amount of money you will need. It's only natural to try and be frugal and optimistic when planning how much money you'll need (or, more likely, how much debt you will have to take on), but our rule of thumb is to figure out how much you *think* you will need—and then add 10 to 20 percent. Remember what we said about undercapitalization often ruining franchises!

The bottom line is that most franchisees put down between 20 to 40 percent of the total cost and finance the rest. Where does this financed money come from? The figures we gathered from the franchisors who responded to the Francorp/DePaul University survey (see Chapter 3) can provide a partial answer. According to this study, 41 percent of respondents provided *some* kind of financing to their franchisees; a substantial number of other franchisors offered no *direct* financing, but instead recommended franchisees to lenders who were likely to be responsive to the franchisees' needs. Other interesting figures gleaned from the responses of these franchisors: 20 to 28 percent of their franchisees receive at least *some* amount of Small Business Administration (SBA) financing; around half of their franchisees tap into the equity in their home; and up to 75 percent of their franchisees pledged personal assets as collateral to obtain a bank loan.

In general, the following seven sources are places to look for franchise financing.

1. **Personal wealth.** Your home(s), car(s), savings, art, jewelry, and other valuables can be used to finance your franchise—but, as we've pointed out, it's best not to go in with your "last dime," in case some level of financial reserves are needed.

2. **"F & F" financing.** F & F stands for family and friends. The advantage of borrowing from these sources (or selling them equity in your franchise) is they know you and—presumably!—like you. The disadvantage is if things go badly, they may like you less later. According to the Francorp/DePaul survey, some 22 percent of franchisees utilize this source of financing.

3. **The franchisor.** The above-cited 41 percent figure is encouraging—and it's 10 percent *higher* than the figure for this question in a previous survey conducted by the same organizations, showing that more franchisors are offering at least some form of financing to their franchisees.

4. **Banks.** In general, straight bank financing has become harder to get for franchisees, but there are financial institutions that do lend to franchisees; a little research

can help boost your chances (especially if that research includes a reference from your franchisor).

5. **Leasing.** This can be a way to obtain equipment, fixtures, and even the business's location; many franchisors have preexisting arrangements with suppliers to assist their new franchisees. The cost of leasing can be high, but it can also reduce your overall debt.

6. **Government sources.** There is usually a considerable amount of "red tape" wrapped around these sources of money—such as SBA or equivalent state-agency loans—but they *can* be worth investigating.

7. **Venture capital and/or limited partnerships.** This solution is usually confined to very large investments, such as an entire franchising territory. In return, you will likely have to give up a big chunk of equity, but most franchisors require you to retain more than 50 percent of the franchise ownership.

After securing financing, the final immediate step before the close is the mostly precautionary process of having your legal and accounting professionals review the contracts and figures, a step we call "bringing in the pros."

Bringing in the Pros

We give close scrutiny to a variety of franchising legal matters (including giving detailed answers to some frequently asked questions) in Chapter 9; and we'll state here an important-to-remember point we repeat there: At this stage, you should have your personal attorney (or business attorney, if you have one) look over the offering circular and, especially, the franchise agreement. However, we make that suggestion with the following caveat: The material points included in these documents are almost universally *not* negotiable. Your attorney will not be involved in drafting these documents or negotiating compromises on their component points, but will rather provide you with guidance and advice; the same holds true for your accountant, if you wish to use one to go over the numbers involved (this is always a good idea). This advice can be valuable, but by now you should know far more about the franchisor than any advisor could glean by a quick look at these documents, so be sure to weigh any objections against what you already know (and feel). But if these professional advisors strenuously object to points or terms that the franchisor cannot clearly and respectfully justify to your satisfaction, perhaps you shouldn't go with this particular franchisor.

One final point on professional advisors: Be sure to agree on the "scope of engagement" in advance. That is, make it clear what you want them to do and what you *don't* want, and get a good idea of the cost involved. For example, you don't want your attorney to start rewriting parts of the franchise agreement, just to tell you if he sees serious problems with any of its provisions.

Perhaps the Longest Two Weeks You Will Ever Spend

Suppose that, on meeting with a franchisor, you decide to buy the franchise. The ten-business-day waiting period before you can actually sign the agreement can go one of two ways—either it will pass relatively quickly, with very little apprehension, because you feel good and secure about a decision to buy, or it can drag, with doubts growing each day until you're not sure if you want to go through with the whole thing. If the latter is the case, maybe you *don't* want to go through with it; when push comes to shove, maybe franchising just *isn't* right for you, no matter your test score in Chapter 3. If this is true, it's better to find out now (even considering the amount you may have spent to discover it), than to feel trapped into committing even more time and money to what will likely be a failure or (at best) an unenjoyable under-taking.

But just because you feel nervous doesn't necessarily mean that you've made the wrong decision. At least some amount of "buyer's remorse" is normal with a purchase or investment of this magnitude. If you *do* feel overly anxious about the decision, review the reasons why you thought it was a *good* decision. Talk to the franchisor's representative (you'll likely hear from him anyway during this period!) and ask specific questions about things you may feel nervous or unclear about. But most of all, look *within* yourself and ask, "Is this the right thing for me to do now?" And, after all the mental hemming and hawing that is likely to accompany this question, if the answer is still yes, get your checkbook ready and move on to the next—and final!—step in this long process.

The Close

If everything is as it should be—from your desire to be in (and your aptitude for) the franchisor's line of business to complete and properly drafted paperwork—the next step is simply to execute the aforementioned documents, write a check to the franchisor, and shake hands. But first . . .

When it comes time to sign the check and make the ultimate decisions, your emotions will likely come into play. Do you feel comfortable with everything? This *definitely* is the time to ask any questions—not *after* you've signed on and paid up (of course, you'll have many questions then, but right now we're referring to basic, fundamental questions that should affect your overall decision).

And then, after any last-minute questions have been an-swered, you *are* ready. Your hand may be a bit unsteady, but remember this: With all the advice you have received and all the research you did, your *decision* should be pretty steady by now. So sign on the dotted line, and get ready for the adventure you've been looking forward to. You are now a franchisee!

Time for a Deep Breath

It's been a *long* journey—three chapters worth for us; countless hours of reading, research, and decision making for you. Time for a break. Before we go on to the franchisor-oriented chapters, we're going to share some interesting stories and valuable advice from real-life franchisors and franchisees in the next chapter.

But before we do, Joe tells a story about the emotions which can surface during "the close." Joe was advising a friend about a franchise and visited the headquarters with the friend for the final step in the process. The friend stopped to use the men's room at the franchisor's office, and when he returned, he said to Joe, "That's it. Let's go—this is not for me." Joe was surprised, as everything appeared rosy on the surface.

On the way back to the airport the friend related the happenings in the men's room that ultimately sunk the sale. Apparently, the friend heard two salesmen talking about another potential franchisee, debating when they should make their move to "jerk the check."

While this may be acceptable casual lingo for salespeople, overhearing it created such a poor impression in Joe's friend that it completely turned off a person who might have made a good franchisee!

Voices of Experience: Profiles of Successful Franchisees and Franchisors

Throughout this book we have cautioned that before making any franchising decision you should obtain as much relevant information as you can. Particularly, you should receive this information from people whose experiences can be meaningful to you. As a prospective franchisee, this means talking to existing franchisees of the franchisor (or franchisors) you are considering. As a prospective franchisor, you should gather intelligence from competitive franchisors, if you can, and franchisors in other fields, if you can't. But don't assume if you're planning to franchise, say, a pet supplies store, you should not contact successful pet supply franchisors and ask for advice and opinions. In our experience, people often are surprisingly candid in this situation—just when you might expect them to be secretive or suspicious.

In this chapter, as a brief and informative interlude in our detailed examination of the steps involved in becoming a franchisee and franchisor, we offer the results of some interviews of our own. You'll read what both franchisees and franchisors say about how and why they got into business, and what they would do differently if they had it to do over again. Remember, there is no need to reinvent the wheel as you enter franchising. Learn from these examples, and save your energy for other challenges and/or problems.

YOUTH AND AMBITION:

Tina Mondazzi, Copies Now franchisee

Tina is both representative of today's franchisees—young, bright, enthusiastic—and also very much a unique case. She bought her first Copies Now franchise when she was twenty-four; two years later, she bought her second outlet, got it going, and has recently sold it. (Copies Now offers color copying, high-speed duplicating, and desktop publishing; it is a division of Sir Speedy.) Not yet thirty, she is already a successful franchisee and ready for a variety of new challenges.

Why Did You Choose Franchising?

"I wanted to open a business. I knew I could be as successful for myself as I had been for other people as an employee or consultant. I liked the copying/printing business, and Sir Speedy seemed to be the most aggressive and market-driven franchise in the field. I spent some eight months researching what I wanted and lining up my financing (the strength of franchising in general made that easier to get). I was literally ready to open my store a month after deciding to go with Copies Now.

"The only problem was at first they didn't want to approve where I wanted to put my store—in Enfield, Connecticut, a suburban, 'bedroom' community about twenty miles north of Hartford. I wanted the store there because I lived there, saw more

122

business services coming into this market, and, quite honestly, because I didn't feel like driving farther! (Between construction and commuting, the highways around here are usually a mess.) It got to the point where my location in Enfield was either going to be my Copies Now franchise or an independent Tina's Copy Center. Finally, I convinced them I could make a go of it in Enfield—and, after my first year, I won Copies Now's 'Rookie of the Year' award for highest sales of any new franchisee that year.

"Now, I admit that that isn't necessarily the *best* way to get into franchising. It takes lots of courage and confidence to do it the way I did it. But it worked for me."

(Author's note: Franchise location is obviously a very central issue to your long-term success. There are a number of businesses which specialize in the selection of good retail locations for different types of businesses. We are not just talking about real estate brokers, but companies that factor in all the proper demographics and traffic counts and do a nice statistically based job of analysis. One company we have found to be excellent—and there are others—is Steven Greenberg, The Greenberg Group, 1200 W. Broadway #6, Hewlett, NY 11557, 516-295-0406.)

How Are You Different from Many Franchisees?

"Two years after my first store opened, I bought a second store, in Vernon, Connecticut. I admit I was a little bored after making the first store a success, and since I wasn't working the counter— although I was running the store's day-to-day operations—I wanted to find a new challenge. After I bought the second store and got it running, I realized it wasn't the answer to my needs. The most gratifying thing about the second store was making the deal and getting the store open and running. So I sold it.

"Doing that rather than building a continuing portfolio of more stores probably makes me different than many franchisees; there are other things as well, such as my age and my sex. But I feel that the biggest difference between me and most franchisees at the same level of investment is this: It seems many of them are career changers who are leaving the corporate world, and who have family members working at the franchise or helping support the venture with a second paycheck. For them, owning a franchise is the culmination of their dream of being their own boss—even though they may build that dream into a minichain of franchised outlets. For me, franchising is just the beginning. I used the strength of franchising to secure bank financing for my business, and I built my stores into successes. I'm keeping my first store, but it's a solid block for me to build from, not my sole priority. I thought I would like being a Copies Now franchisee— and I do—but I never thought it would be the only thing I would do. And it won't be.

"I'm currently exploring public relations and marketing and trying to help others market their businesses. I recently began college; owning my own business has finally allowed me both the time and money to get a degree! I have achieved success through franchising, but I am continuing to grow—as a person and as a businesswoman—and plan to achieve success in other areas."

Advice and Thoughts about Franchising

"I feel that franchisees are given an opportunity that they must then capitalize on. The franchisor gives you information, helps set you up, and then, even considering the assistance and advice available from the franchisor, it's up to *you* to succeed. The difference between a successful and an unsuccessful franchisee is what you do *after* the franchisor sets you up.

"I think it's also important that franchising provides a support structure and a forum that you can't find any other place. You can ask questions (of the franchisor or of other franchisees) and feel confident that you will get real answers that will help you in real situations."

A FRANCHISE AS AN INVESTMENT:

J. L. Jackson, Valvoline Instant Oil Change franchisee

J. L. is a successful businessman headquartered in Dallas. He is the former president and chief operating officer of Diamond Shamrock

Corporation (from which he took early retirement in 1987) and a longtime oil, gas, and coal man in Texas and Kentucky. He remains active as a board member and/or a director of a number of universities, corporations, and civic organizations. His investments include real estate holdings, stocks and bonds, and a Valvoline Instant Oil Change franchise in Florida.

How Did You Get into Franchising?

"After taking early retirement from Diamond Shamrock, I began looking into franchise opportunities as potential investments. Some of the opportunities I examined were in the food field, but in general—probably because my business background was so different from food service—I was not as comfortable with these as I would like to have been. A big problem inherent in some of the franchises I researched was they were relatively new ideas— new segments within their own field—or new franchisors. My concern was if the franchisor wasn't stable financially and operationally they could fail. And if the franchisor failed, usually the franchisee would too! So I was interested in a franchise more in tune with my background and experiences and one in which I could feel confident.

"I also believed that, with today's busy two-paycheck families, any service that could save time and give people more time for leisure and family pursuits had a good chance to be successful. These lines of thought led me to Valvoline Instant Oil Change. When Ashland Oil, Valvoline's parent company, decided to franchise a quick oil-change operation, I was very interested, because I was familiar with Ashland's management and knew it was very stable. After investigating their expansion into franchising, I felt they had a long-term commitment to the success of this system—it wasn't just a fad.

"In 1989, after considerable discussions with Valvoline/ Ashland, I and a longtime friend and business associate, Robert Mayes, from Lexington, Kentucky, bought a Valvoline area development franchise. We were most interested in locating our franchise in Texas or Kentucky—areas we knew best—but Valvoline's research and demographics led us instead to Jacksonville, Florida. Our minimum area commitment is for three stores; we have one open, the second under construction, and are currently negotiating a site for the third. My partner's son, Scott Mayes, is our on-site manager, and he will likely continue in this role—with other levels of management to be created below him—as we complete our second and third outlets and look toward further development of our territory.

"It's more of an investment for me than a job. It was weeks after our first shop opened before I even set foot in it! But, as with any other investment, I did my homework beforehand. I was confident that this was a solid concept and a good investment."

What Advice Would You Give to Prospective Franchisees?

"The biggest concern I would express to someone considering buying a franchise is the same one that faced me: Is the franchisor—no matter the field—established, reputable, and, especially, well funded?

"I would tell a prospective franchisee to look for a franchisor who has demonstrated the ability to fully understand its line of business and who has the resources to provide full service and support to its franchisees. No matter how hot the idea, I feel the franchisor's honesty and basic ability are among the most important factors in selecting a franchise . . . I wouldn't be where I am with Valvoline today if I hadn't known them as well as I did."

Thoughts on Franchising

"I feel that many successful franchises—and more and more of the future franchises that *will* be successful—are those that fill the niche of convenience and time saving. Today's families have less time together, and any well-run business that can save them time—be it by providing fast food, home-cleaning services, or quick oil changes—has a good chance at succeeding. I think franchised businesses are a very good way to serve these needs.

"Also, for people like myself who are able to invest more money, but not necessarily more time, into a larger operation, using franchising can be a good way to benefit from the

experience of the franchisor and avoid some of the time and
energy spent going through the basic learning curve of a new
business."

"MOM AND POP" IN THE BABY BUSINESS:
Margaret and Richard Mayr, USA Baby franchisees

The classic profile of owner-operated franchises is the married
couple that runs the business together. Often it works well;
sometimes it doesn't. The Mayrs are a success story. He's a former
independent trucker; she was formerly in operations and marketing with AT&T in New York City. Their overlapping travel
schedules meant they hardly saw each other, so they decided to
start a business together. After much careful research they moved
to West Hartford, Connecticut, and opened a USA Baby store in
June 1988. (Incidentally, this is your chance to hear both sides of
the story—USA Baby's experience as a franchisor is profiled later
in this chapter!)

How Did You Get into Franchising?
"We did a lot of demographic research before we even decided
what business we wanted to be in. We had a million things in our
heads at first. We actually knew one of the principals of USA
Baby through family connections and mentioned our plans to him
at a wedding. He suggested we look at their franchise. Richie
managed to get an assignment to deliver a load of freight to their
headquarters, and visited some stores while he was there. He
liked what he saw, so we traveled to Chicago for a meeting with
the franchisor. They were very honest; they told us it's not easy to
own a business and were up-front about the risks involved. We
appreciated that.

"The more we got behind the scenes of running a business,
the more we knew we needed a franchise rather than going it
alone. Neither of us had any experience with advertising or retail
operations. It's funny, but finding out the mistakes our franchisors

had made actually encouraged us; it meant we could avoid making the same mistakes.

"Looking back, there's no way we could have done it alone. The sales reps for some manufacturers wouldn't even have opened us up as accounts, while as franchisees we not only buy from them, we buy at special pricing. One store starting out by itself just couldn't survive the competition. Especially during the recession, having professional advertising really helped set us apart. We also have some exclusive items that people can't get anywhere else and therefore can't price-shop."

What Has It Been Like, Being in Business with a Spouse?

Margaret laughs. "Some of our friends wonder; they say, 'If it were us, we'd kill each other.' But we've found it has actually strengthened our marriage. If anything, it's let us know that we can survive stress together! Seriously, we try to stay out of each other's hair: Richie has the warehouse and receiving, while I handle most of the administration and ordering. And we both enjoy working with customers. Actually, our office is so tiny that we can't both be in there at the same time for long, which helps!

"If a couple had a problem with their marriage going in, owning a business would probably just make it worse, but we've learned when we have to disagree we should just get it out, get it over, and move on. Our only major problem is trying not to talk business *all* the time when we're at home!"

What Is the Most Satisfying Thing about Owning a Franchise?

"Two things: the flexibility and the sense of accomplishment. Flexibility really became important when Kathryn was born and Margaret needed to take time off now and then. After she came back to work she put Kathryn into a Snuggli or a playpen right out of our stock, and Kathryn was practically part of the staff till she started walking.

"The sense of accomplishment is increasing as our customers

come back shopping for things for their second or third children. It means they liked what they got when they were here before. We're negotiating right now to rent an additional 3,000 square feet of space, so we can put in a line of furniture for older children. That's an idea we've had for a while, but the seeds were planted by our franchisor and a couple of the other franchisees.

"Being a part of a franchise has been very important. Any time we've had a problem or question the guys at the home office are right there on the phone for us. And we've enjoyed getting together with other franchise owners and sharing ideas. They have similar experiences but aren't competitors, so we can talk freely. We give and we get."

Any Major Disappointments?

"Not disappointments exactly, but it does take its toll in terms of time. That's like any other business, I guess. It's the flip side of being the boss: You're flexible, but you're also responsible for everything. The night before the first day we opened for business, we were both worrying about it till three A.M. We kept asking each other, 'Are you still awake?' If we had nine-to-five jobs we could just go home and leave them behind sometimes, but you can't do that when you're the owner."

What Advice Would You Give to Prospective Franchisees?

"Do your research and plan carefully. Despite all the things franchisors will tell you, ultimately you have to make the decision yourself. And don't run out of money; it will probably take more than you think."

CORPORATE DROPOUT:

Jim Jackson, PIP Printing franchisee

Jim actually represents two important categories of franchisees—executives who have left the corporate world and minorities. He is an African-American with a very diverse background—he taught school; served a term in the Iowa House of Representatives; joined Pepsi as a regional representative and ended up as a vice president and general manager of a bottling operation; worked for ITT as a liaison between field operations and corporate headquarters and Citibank; and had six separate subsidiaries reporting to him at Cigna. He left Cigna in 1988 at age forty-nine and he became a PIP Printing franchisee while pursuing his dream of becoming a franchisor!

How Did You Get into Franchising?

"I had experience being my own boss and I liked that. So after I left Cigna, I formed my own company, QPC, which provides child care centers—called Kids' Corner—on or near corporate campuses. We have several locations we own or manage, and I planned to expand Kids' Corner into a franchise. I am still working toward becoming a franchisor. But in 1988, while establishing Kids' Corner, I had occasion to use a printer. I patronized a PIP Printing franchise, and the business caught my interest. I realized that they were a growing company who were adapting their entire business concept from copying to business printing to meet the changing needs of their customers and industry. I looked into several other printing franchises, but was most comfortable with PIP. One reason was because it offered general corporate structures and planning concepts that were similar to those I had experienced with the successful corporations for which I had worked. Also, the evolution of their business convinced me they were progressive and would continue to grow and adapt.

"When investigating PIP, one of my biggest concerns was technical and operational support. I knew how to run a business, but did *not* particularly know how to run a printing business. I needed to be sure they would help me do it. They convinced me that the support I needed was actively—not just theoretically—in place. And I visited several franchisees to confirm this.

"I wanted a large enough market, but not one that I felt was oversupplied. I was given an area development in Chicago (I have one store open and will develop four more stores in a total of five years). The market was certainly large enough, but I was concerned that the competition might be overwhelming. Now I'm convinced that the marketing efforts of my various competitors leave me enough room to carve out my niche."

If You Were Starting Over, What Would You Do Differently?

"There are two things I would do, perhaps not *differently,* but certainly with more intensity: (1) I would focus more on providing quality product and service. I strongly believe in this, and we did strive for it, but I'd pay even more attention to it if I was starting again. The satisfied repeat customer is the best customer in the world. And (2) I'd pay a hell of a lot more attention to the financial services package—on keeping an eye on how the business is doing from month to month. It's important to scrupulously collect, disseminate, and analyze financial information. These two steps must be in place first to help lead to successes in other areas of the business."

How is Franchising Helping You Achieve Your Dream?

"Getting into PIP was an outgrowth of my ultimate dream of providing high-quality child care. Developing Kids' Corner was the catalyst of my becoming a franchisee in general and a PIP franchisee in particular. I think I can better understand both sides of the franchisor/franchisee relationship having been a franchisee while beginning to develop my franchisor program. I have been in the corporate world as a manager and an executive, having worked for franchisors, i.e. Pepsi and ITT (with its franchise-oriented divisions, Canteen Corporation and Sheraton), and now as a franchisee with PIP. And I think all this experience has made me a good franchisee and will make me an even better franchisor."

What Advice Would You Give to Prospective Franchisees?

"My advice is in four parts: (1) Find an area that will be fun—you'll work very hard with long hours, so you had better like it! (2) If you're not committed to quality, don't bother—no matter what the field. (3) When it comes to choosing a particular franchisor, realize that you don't know everything, so make sure you go with a franchisor who can support your areas of weakness. Make sure that the franchisor has the resources—the experience, the financial background—to provide (and to *continue* providing) this assistance to you. And (4) choose a franchisor who demonstrates that they are researching or otherwise planning to implement new products and services to meet the future needs of your franchise. Your franchise will have to adapt to future changes, and the franchisor should be driving such efforts."

Thoughts about Franchising

"I believe that in the marketing of certain products and services, a properly trained owner-manager will usually produce better results than a professional employee-manager. The incentive is higher, and consequently, so is the quality of the product/service. Franchising is the best way I know to achieve this implementation of motivated owner-managers.

"I've been happy to be in franchising as a franchisee, and I look forward to selling my first franchise as a franchisor."

BOTH SIDES OF FRANCHISING:

Murry Evans, Burger King franchisee and Signs Now franchisor

Murry has spent time on both sides of the franchising fence. Since 1962, this modest, self-effacing, deeply religious millionaire has been a Burger King franchisee, watching his mini-empire grow to forty-four stores in Alabama, Florida, Mississippi, Tennessee, and

Texas. He bought the Signs Now franchise system in 1986 (it started in 1983). The franchises of this chain produce computer-generated signs, vehicle lettering, banners, and magnetic signs in twenty-four hours or less. In the next five years he expanded the chain from less than ten units to more than 120. After achieving great success as a franchisee, he is duplicating that success as a franchisor while helping to provide others with the opportunities that he has been given.

How Did You Become a Franchisee?
"Basically, it all began when I ate a Whopper and thought it was the best burger I ever ate. I was sold on the product and later on the people. I checked out the franchisees—back then, no one told me that I *should* be doing this—and visited the chain's headquarters in Miami. And I was convinced that this was a solid, successful operation.

"I borrowed $40,000, which was a lot of money in 1962, from my father-in-law, a frugal Ohio farmer. It wasn't easy to convince him. It took about six to eight months of taking him to Burger Kings, and after seeing it and tasting the food and hearing me plead, he said, 'Okay, Murry, I'll lend you the money.' I just about fell over! And he told me why he thought it was a good investment. 'This is not a fad.' Well, that didn't mean as much to me then, but I always remembered what he said."

How Did You Become a Franchisor?
"After my experience with Burger King, I knew that franchising was the best way to build a business. Signs Now was like Burger King was when it started out—it was new and on the leading edge of a growing field. I visited a store and spent time with the people involved. While doing this research, I remembered my father-in-law's point—and I asked myself if this was a fad. The question meant a little more to me when it was *my* money. I knew that, as a business owner, when I wanted a sign—such as a banner for my Burger Kings—I wanted it immediately, but often had to wait a week or more. But, with Signs Now, customers could have

signs in twenty-four hours. I decided, like my father-in-law had about Burger King, that it was a solid business, and not a fad.

"I knew the company had the ability to grow, but it didn't have the money it needed to achieve its place in the marketplace. I knew *I* could make it work, so I bought the company. And now I have the opportunity to give people a chance as franchisees, just like *I* was given a chance. I like the fact that I am able to offer a business opportunity that can help other enthusiastic, hard-working people make money."

What Advice Would You Give to Prospective Franchisors?

"I'd tell them it's tougher and more expensive than people might think. It takes money to do it right—hamburgers, signs, *whatever* the business is. And, in addition to relatively deep pockets, you need to have the right people, the right skills, and a proven concept. I think you should have successful units—preferably, more than one—before you attempt to franchise."

What Advice Would You Give to Prospective Franchisees?

"Find a new industry that is ready to grow. Search out a franchisor who is steady financially and has good, bright personnel in place. Talk to its existing franchisees. You should feel confident the franchisor has a future before you commit *your* future to it. I think that mature industries can be too hard to break into—why play against the big boys? You need to be able to achieve an optimum return on your investment, and a new industry gives you the best opportunity to do that."

Thoughts about Franchising

"I don't want to change—I don't want to sell my Burger Kings. I'm happy as both a franchisor and franchisee. If I'd gone into Murry's Burgers twenty-nine years ago, I might have lasted a year or two or maybe even five or six, but I wouldn't be where I am today.

"Franchising has been the wave of the past and it's still the wave of the future. It's a proven method to market products and services. I think that franchising is absolutely the way to go."

PIONEER FRANCHISOR:

Jules Lederer, former Budget Rent A Car franchisor

Jules is one of franchising's elder statesmen. His Budget Rent A Car was the first nationwide discount car rental chain and was a franchising contemporary of such other early successes as McDonald's, Holiday Inns, and Kentucky Fried Chicken. From its franchising start in 1960, Budget grew to more than five hundred worldwide franchisees in 1968 when the company was sold to Transamerica. He remains active as a businessman and an occasional consultant on franchising.

How Did You Get into Franchising?

"At the time, I had no experience in either car rental or in franchising. In 1960, when I started franchising, what I knew about the field would fit on the head of a pin. I didn't have a clue. But what I had was a solid sales and marketing background, and a desire for a new challenge.

"In 1958, a cousin of mine opened a rental-car office in Los Angeles with forty-eight used cars and a plan to undercut the prices charged by Hertz and Avis. I told him that his name—Budget—and his concept seemed like winners, but that I thought he needed new cars to appeal to the largest number of people. I bankrolled the company's first one hundred new autos, and discount car rental—using new cars—was born.

"We established our niche in the marketplace, often without competing head to head with the other car-rental companies. Most of their offices were located at major airport terminals, but we weren't. We were near the airport, but also near residential and commercial areas, so we were appealing to more than just travelers. After two years of success, the company was ready for expansion. But I knew I didn't have the money to expand Budget through traditional corporate channels. I just couldn't afford to go after Hertz and Avis on my own. My friend, Kemmons Wilson, suggested that I expand Budget the same way that Wilson and his partner expanded Holiday Inns—through franchising. It seemed logical that sharing the knowledge we had acquired with enthusiastic franchisees, who would invest time and money in their franchises, was the most viable way to expand Budget."

If You Were Starting Over, What Would You Do Differently?

"I had virtually no knowledge of franchising when I began. For example, I originally used Avis as a model to set up Budget's royalty structure. The royalties were set at flat amounts which did not grow into larger percentages as each outlet grew. This cost Budget a considerable sum. I consider this cost the 'tuition' for my education in franchising. Franchise consulting firms didn't exist then. In retrospect, the fee for experienced guidance would have cost me far less than those first mistakes did."

What Advice Would You Give a Prospective Franchisor?

"There are three points that I think any fledgling franchisor should follow: (1) Have a valid, well-defined concept that has proven itself and has universal appeal. (2) Select qualified, enthusiastic, and financially able franchisees. If you grant a franchise to someone who is short of money, and he ends up failing because of this, not only do you lose his flow of royalties, but the failure can also hurt your franchise's reputation. And (3) provide sufficient training and support. The relationship between the franchisor and franchisee is basically parental: The franchisee places his trust—and money—with the franchisor, and, in return, he must receive guidance. Both parties must be determined to make it work."

Thoughts on Franchising Today

"I think that the size and quality of today's pool of franchisee prospects is unprecedented in recent history. Back in the 1960s, when Budget was first franchising, I used to dream of the day when prospective franchise buyers would have the capital and business experience that today's prospects have."

SELLING YOUR EXPERTISE:

Al Levine, USA Baby/The Baby's Room franchisor

Al worked his way up from selling juvenile furniture door to door. Since opening his first store with partner Vincent Powell in a Chicago suburb in 1975, he has built the leading franchise chain in his field. Known as both USA Baby and The Baby's Room (in different areas), this solid franchise has almost fifty units—most franchised—in twenty-one states. In 1991, *Furniture Today* magazine named USA Baby one of the top one hundred chains, not just in baby furniture but in furniture retailing as a whole.

How Did You Get into Franchising?

"At first, we expanded in corporate-owned stores. But it became apparent that the logistics of nationwide expansion (personnel, finances, etc.) was an obstacle. After successfully supplying management consulting services to independent retailers in our field, we realized that we were practically 'giving away the store' by selling these services, but not collecting royalties on the resultant higher sales these outlets were realizing. Therefore, we decided to go to franchising—through both opening new outlets and converting existing retailers."

If You Were Starting Over, What Would You Do Differently?

"When you start out as a franchisor, you are usually very anxious to get some startups, and consequently, you are sometimes not as selective as you might be and perhaps *should* be. Hindsight is easy, but, as our franchise program has matured, we've become more selective, in terms of capitalization and in terms of personality. Back when we started, we were more lenient—now we're more careful. Still, when I think back about the franchisees we signed, and I wonder, 'Would I have still signed so-and-so, knowing what I know now?' the answer is probably yes. But being as selective as you can afford to be helps both parties.

"Many franchisees—even at our higher level of investment ($200,000)—are a bit naive. They see we are a successful chain, and they want to be part of that success. They feel that they can do it and they want to do it. You hardly have to sell these individuals on becoming a franchisee. But is it best for both the franchisor *and* the franchisee? Because if it isn't, it may hurt the franchisee more than the franchisor.

"Getting one more franchise fee is *not* what we're trying to do. We're trying to build a successful organization. It's great to be able to say you have two hundred or some other large number of franchisees, but they have to be solid. These franchisees have to have enough capital to get through any tough times."

Have You Realized Your Dream Through Franchising?

"Basically, yes. We've taken franchising and proven that it works for us. And we've reached a plateau of sorts. We've gotten to this point and we want to spend the next few years heading toward the next step, which would be one hundred outlets. It'll take a larger organization, more people, and a changing corporate structure, but we're ready to move ahead. I think most entrepreneurs would tell you that they're not satisfied with where they are, and our intent is to keep on growing."

What Advice Would You Give a Prospective Franchisor?

"I feel strongly that you should seek the help and experience of professionals. I *have* had people ask me for advice, and I enthusiastically refer them to Don's firm, who helped us get started. Can you get into franchising cheaper than through a full-service consulting firm? Sure. But can you get it done better and more thoroughly? In my opinion, no.

"I would also tell potential franchisors to realize that they are about to be in a separate business. I learned very quickly that selling baby furniture and selling franchises were two *very* different businesses. You can't try to sell franchises as a sideline. It needs the full attention of yourself or of the people you hire to run it. If you don't treat your franchise program as a separate business from your original business, I feel that you will probably not be successful at franchising."

Thoughts on Franchising

"Franchising is only going to get stronger. I think that someone who wants to start their own business today has to be out of their mind if they don't go into franchising. It's important to do your homework, and determine the best path for your business or for you personally, but I think that franchising has something to offer almost everyone—potential franchisors and franchisees alike."

TAKING A NEW CONCEPT TO THE TOP—FAST:

Ron Matsch, Discovery Zone franchisor

Ron is one of the latest success stories in franchising. An expert in recreational design and facility management (with a special interest in general fitness), he founded Discovery Zone with Al Fong, an Olympics gymnastics coach. They began franchising this fun fitness center aimed at children—sort of a safe and educational indoor playground—in the fall of 1990, and, by the end of 1991, had already sold approximately 106 franchises. (Tennis great Billie Jean King is a franchisee and corporate investor.) As the baby boomlet of baby boomers having children continues to grow, he sees the market for his innovative franchise as also continuing to grow.

How Did You Get into Franchising?

"I had been in the sports business for years, and I wanted something to keep kids active and teach them about fitness in a fun way. I have two young children, so they're a major part of the reason I developed this concept. Al and I bought some forty cans of Tinkertoys and built a small model of the equipment setup that we thought would both appeal to and benefit the kids. For example, if you show kids a pull-up bar, it's fairly boring to them, but show them our colorful vinyl mountain that they can climb with ropes, and it's fun—but the same exercise is achieved. I refer to Discovery Zone as 'the broccoli that tastes good.' It's fun *and* good for them. I think it fills the need to get kids away from television and for kids and parents to spend good, fun time together.

"We decided that franchising was the best way to get the most locations open in the shortest amount of time. This way, our expertise could be duplicated through systems and training, and our operators wouldn't have to have specialized experience in fitness or health areas. And it would be less capital-intensive than trying to open individual corporate-owned outlets.

"Our decision to franchise was pretty fundamental. We thought Discovery Zone was a good business and had the potential to be profitable. We wanted a national—and, eventually, an international—presence as fast as possible. Franchising allowed us to do this while maintaining the level of quality that we felt was an integral part of our business."

Have You Realized Your Dream Through Franchising?

"The rewards have been great in seeing people become able to own and operate their own business. Personally, it's been exciting to exceed the original first-year goals set in our business plan. The next stage of our dream is to go international—kids are kids, regardless of nationality or background. We have set our goals high and have achieved phenomenal success thus far."

What Advice Would You Give Prospective Franchisors?

"I would tell them to get a good consultant—someone who can analyze and make sure your business has all the right components. We did some research and found a good consultant. Professional guidance can ensure that you properly develop all aspects of your franchise business.

"I also think that franchisors need to establish a good budget designed to help grow the business until it can be supported solely by royalties. A critical factor is that franchisors have to have a good system and staff in place *before* the growth period, to better capitalize on it when it does come. You have to be prepared to spend a significant amount of capital for a down-the-road payoff."

Thoughts on Franchising

"It's been said many times, but I believe that franchising continues to be the wave of the future. A common dream is to be able to own your own business, but very few people have the legal, accounting, and operational background to do this successfully. Franchising can help provide the best vehicle to achieve this dream. The franchisor provides assistance and expertise that can cover weaknesses or inexperience the franchisees may have.

"For example, our franchisees don't have to have doctorates in physical education or *any* special training in certain fitness fields, but they are able to successfully own and operate a Discovery Zone franchise because we're there to help them."

Postscript

As this book was being readied for the press, Ron's company—with over 200 franchises sold in two years—was purchased by a major Chicago investor, then went public at a valuation of about $600 million. Franchising's rapid growth had again attracted the interest of savvy businesspeople who knew a good deal when they saw it!

THE SECOND TIME AROUND:

Mark Dalen, Silk Plants, Etc. and Silkcorp Factory Outlets

The final voice of our "voices of experience" is a bit different from all that have gone before. It's the voice of Mark Dalen, who achieved success through franchising before and is now trying to do it all over again. Both times, his chosen vehicle was silk plants.

Plants are a high-demand, attractive decorating accessory. The downside is that they require a lot of care—watering, feeding, and pruning—and still often end up brown and wilted on the windowsill. Years ago, Mark Dalen found that well-crafted silk flowers can be even better than the real thing. He founded Silk Plants, Etc., a business that can replace almost any plant with an amazingly lifelike imitation that will never wither. The merchandise selection also includes bridal bouquets, eight-foot-tall trees, floral arrangements, and the brass, ceramic, and wicker pots to put them in.

Even though Mark had worked with plastic, silk, and dried flowers for almost ten years, he was under thirty when he opened his first Silk Plants, Etc. store. As a sole entrepreneur, he developed his own reliable sources of imported materials and finished goods. The company prospered quickly, adding several new locations within its first few years. In 1985, Dalen, responding to requests from people who admired his stores, chose franchising as his principal expansion method. Indeed, he began to sell franchises rapidly as soon as his franchise development program was completed.

But as Silk Plants, Etc. grew to upward of 100 stores, Dalen was confronted with a paradox. To feed his mushrooming chain, he needed large quantities of inventory; to get this inventory, a credit line of literally millions of dollars was required. But Dalen, despite the growth of his company, was unable to obtain that kind of credit. At the same time, he also began to feel the pressures of heavier management concerns than he had ever encountered before. Into the picture stepped a large public company, Ozite Corporation, which offered an amount in excess of $5 million for Silk Plants, Etc. It was an offer Dalen could not refuse, and he sold out, continuing for a time as an officer with the new company. By mid-1987, nearly one-third of the more than 150 Silk Plants, Etc. stores were franchises.

But Mark was too young to retire. A few years later, when his noncompete agreement with Ozite expired, Dalen was ready with a new silk-plant concept. This time, he decided to latch onto the boom in deep-discount merchandising. He created a much bigger store offering a veritable "jungle" of silk plants in a "factory outlet" setting. He cut prices to the bone by buying in bulk and actually assembling the plants in or near each store.

Public response showed that the years hadn't dulled Mark Dalen's instincts for marketing; Silkcorp Factory Outlet was an immediate success. As soon as the concept had proven itself, Mark started to franchise, and was in the process of marketing and selling his first franchises as this book went to press.

Repeating a success in business is often a difficult challenge. But judging by Mark Dalen's track record—and that of franchising—we suspect that he'll succeed all over again. Silk Plants, Etc., franchisees were typically middle managers from large organizations, whose entrepreneurial spirit had been stifled and who wanted a unique business opportunity. The ranks of prospective franchisees fitting that description have swelled in the nineties due to corporate downsizing and layoffs. Silkcorp and Mark Dalen are out to prove that a strongly stated business philosophy of commitment to quality merchandise, low prices, and franchise support will be as attractive to aspiring business owners in the nineties as it was in the eighties.

Conclusion

These educational and interesting voices of experience offer differing opinions and points of view, but their real-world observations on franchising are indeed valuable to novice franchisees and franchisors alike.

Tina, J. L., Margaret and Richard, Jim, Murry, Jules, Al, Ron, and Mark have come from a variety of backgrounds and have chosen franchising for a variety of reasons, yet all readily acknowledge and endorse the power of franchising as a vehicle to achieve business ownership or expansion. They have experienced the advantages that franchising can provide.

We have already explored becoming a franchisee; in the next two chapters we will outline a thorough program for expanding a business through franchising—for becoming a *franchisor*.

Becoming a Franchisor, Part I: Is Your Business Franchisable?

How many hot new ideas are there out there for new franchises? How many brand-new franchises make it to the first grand opening of their very first franchised outlet? Quite a few! Each year, the total number of franchisors increases by an average of 10 to 15 percent. That's some 300 to 450 new, hungry franchisors every year, adding to the established heavy hitters (McDonald's, Holiday Inns, H & R Blocks, et al.)

As a potential franchisor, does all that competition sound challenging? It should. Does it also sound like a challenge you might be up to? Well, if it does, you're in the right place!

Expanding an established business through franchising is anything but a sure bet, but for the right business, properly prepared, franchising can be a successful and rewarding route.

However, if you're considering franchising as a means of expanding your business, there's more you need to know—more about other methods of expansion, more about the various disadvantages of franchising, more about your own business, and more about *yourself.*

In this chapter, you will look at all of the important preliminary steps that go into deciding whether a business is franchisable or not. But first, we will examine the other, more traditional means of expanding a business, and see how franchising compares to them.

Franchising versus Traditional Means of Business Expansion

There is no question that franchising can help business owners expand their businesses in a short period of time without needing large numbers of employees and a large amount of capital. That statement sums up the three primary advantages franchising has over other methods of business expansion: time, people, and money. (There are also a number of distinct *disadvantages* to franchising; we will cover them in depth later in this chapter.)

Businesses seeking to expand can take a number of routes to reach the level of growth they are targeting. These include partnerships (for an infusion of needed capital), networks of dealers or distributors (to better achieve optimum market penetration), and licensing arrangements (which can generate income with little effort but very little control). Of course, if you are simply looking for capital to help your company grow, you can take out a bank loan (increasing your debt) or sell stock (diluting your ownership). Generally speaking, the most common alternative to franchising a business as a means of expansion is through the traditional method of opening company-owned outlets. It is against this method that we will compare franchising to demonstrate its advantages in the following five areas: (1) upfront costs,

(2) recovering your investment, (3) personnel and management, (4) advertising, and (5) market penetration. All of these relate to the advantages of franchising: money, people, and time.

Upfront Costs (Money)

The traditional "sure sign" a retail business was successful and growing used to be the opening of its second unit, and its third, and so on. The company (or its owner) financed the new growth, oversaw its management and staffing, exercised complete control over the expansion program, and retained all of the profits. For years, adding company-owned units was accepted as the logical method of expanding retail businesses. Until some four decades ago, it was the *only* proven method.

Even with the emergence of business-format franchising, many companies cling to the traditional approach of growth from within. Chief among these are most department-store and grocery chains, both highly complex, usually long established (and, in the case of groceries, low-margin) businesses. Nonetheless, company ownership always comes with inherent limits.

For your business, the cost of adding a new outlet or unit might be $50,000 or it might be $5 million. Can you raise that amount without putting your current operation deeply into hock? And, even if you can, how many units can you afford to fund in the span of a year—or in whatever window of opportunity exists before your competition beats you to the punch? Or are you willing to dilute your ownership to enable your business to expand? If so, how large a piece (or pieces) of your business are you willing to give up to fully achieve your expansion plans?

Reduced to its simplest terms, it becomes apparent that the degree of company-owned expansion that can be achieved in any given period of time is restricted by the amount of cash on hand or able to be raised. For most companies, this is a crippling restriction, causing them to move much more slowly than they otherwise might. And, in the process, that window of opportunity can slam shut.

147

Recovering Your Investment (Money, Again, and Time)

Even if you can afford to expand your business by opening a new company-owned unit, how long can you afford to wait to recover your investment? A business generating $300,000 a year in sales may return a profit of $30,000 to $50,000—against which must be figured the corporate costs of supervising that unit. At that rate, it may take three to five years to recover your investment—and, of course, there's no guarantee this unit won't fail before paying for itself.

By comparison, a franchised unit producing the same revenue may generate an annual royalty of around $15,000 (as well as an upfront franchise fee), with supervisory costs that are a fraction of those for a company-owned unit. (We explain why below.) Also, a percentage of these franchised outlets' sales will be dedicated to buying corporate advertising, which benefits the whole chain. And, all the risk of ownership is borne by the franchise. Of course, when the franchise succeeds, you share in that success. The return of investment is quick because your per-unit investment is low.

Personnel And Management (People)

Finding, keeping, and motivating good local managers on an ongoing basis is a difficult and time-consuming process, as you well know if you've had to do it for even one or two outlets. Imagine multiplying that hassle tenfold or hundredfold, or by however many new outlets you wish to open. The same holds true for workers, who, in many areas of the country, expect a pay rate much higher than the minimum wage (due to the lack of available or willing workers). This process of recruiting and training employees becomes more strained and difficult the farther you expand geographically.

The same is true for the day-to-day management of your headquarters operation. It, too, becomes more complex, unwieldy, and people-heavy as you build a company-owned chain. At the very least, you should expect to add a new layer of bureaucracy to your organization to oversee the new and perhaps far-flung outposts of your chain. At worst, you may find you're spending too much time on growth-related details, and not enough time on actually *running* your business and doing long-term planning and development.

However, expansion is a different story for franchises. First and foremost, franchisees are *not* employees. They must be more extensively trained than a manager would be, but, once trained, they don't need the rigorous supervision or chains of command that corporate employees usually require. That's why a franchised chain is so much cheaper to run than a traditional wholly owned company.

Your role in the day-to-day operation of a franchisee's business is more that of a grandparent than a parent. You will be there to give advice and counsel when needed, but you don't have the day-to-day responsibility (or cost) of direct management.

It is quite common for businesses when they turn to franchising to have previously established several company-owned outlets. When they begin their franchise program, many of these companies sell some of these existing units to their managers. The resulting benefits are threefold: (1) These "sell-offs" can bring an initial infusion of cash (depending upon the deal); (2) the "new" franchisees are already old hands at running the business; and (3) company employees see that loyal workers can be rewarded with potentially lucrative business-ownership opportunities.

A good example of this concept in practice is Sterling Optical, an eyewear business with more than two hundred locations. Until 1987, all of its units had been company owned. That year, in an effort to raise some cash, they began selling off established units as franchises (mainly to the optometrists/ opticians that had managed or worked out of the stores). Not only did the sale and conversion of some thirty units over two years raise more than $3 million, but sales at these outlets shot up (compared both to previous years in the same outlet *and* then-current systemwide figures). The annual sales of these thirty units rose between 25 percent and 32 percent in their first year as franchised outlets. As you may have guessed, after these successes, Sterling Optical turned to franchising even more aggressively.

Advertising Pays Off

"Strength in numbers" is more than a cliché—in franchising, it is a primary advantage. A 1990 University of Toronto study found that franchisees outperform—by as much as *three times*—nonfranchised competitors in terms of sales volume and growth. One major reason, the study found, was the strength of national and regional advertising. A local restaurateur, even the leader in its market, could never afford the kind of local (let alone *national*) advertising presence that *every* local outlet of McDonald's or Domino's or Subway benefits from.

Market Penetration (Time)

Let's assume you have a unique concept, one you've tried and tested locally but which has not been established by any other company nationally. Or suppose another company has made your concept work in another region of the country and you are concerned they will move in to compete against you in your region.

Franchising can not only provide you with a hedge against encroachment by competitors, but can also help establish your company as the clear market leader. Through franchising, a small or medium-size entrepreneur can become the dominant force in a market simply by being there first. And, as a franchise grows, so does the ease with which it can attract potential franchisees. At a certain point of success, the object changes from selling potential franchisees on your strengths to merely separating qualified from unqualified applicants! (Please understand, however, that this is a best-case scenario; it can take many years of success to reach such a level.)

The Benefits of a Balanced Mix

All of the above advantages of franchised units over company-owned units is not to imply that company-owned units are an evil or completely unworkable concept. Nearly all of today's top franchisors (excluding, for the most part, conversion franchisors) operate a significant number of company-owned units. The total of company-owned outlets for large franchisors can typically range from 15 to 30 percent of their total units, though much less for certain businesses, especially if service-oriented. In the service-oriented categories of travel and entertainment, construction and maintenance (including house-cleaning services), and laundry and dry cleaning franchises, company-owned units account for only 2 to 5 percent of total outlets. (On the other hand, some franchisors have as many or even *more* company-owned outlets than franchised outlets, but approximately 25 percent is a fairly accurate average.)

Many franchisors find that this balance gives them the best of both worlds: Their franchised units help penetrate a variety of markets quickly and incur little corporate cost; their company-owned units supply a dedicated stream of income as well as acting as "model" stores that can be shown off to both potential *and* existing franchisees as examples of correctly run and successful outlets.

Possible Disadvantages of Franchising Your Business

Franchising *can* mean quick, relatively inexpensive growth for a wide variety of businesses. But for all of its inherent advantages, there can also be counted definite disadvantages. As we noted in Chapter 1, franchising isn't for every business or every businessperson. In some fields, such as businesses with inherently low sales volumes, small profit margins, or high-ticket prices, franchising doesn't work as smoothly as in others. And even in fields in which franchising *has* proven itself, there are certain cases—due to local competition or pricing, for example—where it just doesn't work.

The time to be aware of these potential drawbacks is *now*, not when you're six months and thousands of dollars (if not more) into your fledgling program. Any of the five examples of problems noted below can present themselves to even the best-planned franchise programs (1) loss of direct control, (2) poor franchise performance, (3) finding qualified franchisees, (4) keeping franchisees, and (5) managing rapid growth. Let's look at all of these and how to analyze and deal with each one.

Loss of Direct Control

The biggest single drawback to franchising—and the one that causes the most frustration and anxiety among entrepreneurs who launch franchise programs—is perceived loss of control. Strictly speaking, these aren't going to be *your* stores anymore. The name you chose (perhaps even *your* name) is on the door, and the system in use is the one you developed, but these outlets are your *franchisees'* businesses, and you have to give them the room they need to grow and succeed.

Of course, if franchisees are wreaking havoc with the concept or not living up to reasonable company standards, you will contractually have an avenue of redress, and if the infraction is severe enough or persistent, you will even be able to remove the franchisee. But not every bit of deviation from the norm is mutiny. Some franchisee-implemented modifications can end up benefitting the franchise program as a whole. In the case of McDonald's, the Filet O' Fish sandwich, the Big Mac, and the Egg McMuffin are all popular products that were developed by individual franchisees for their particular markets before being accepted by and, eventually, rolled out to the entire system.

Some entrepreneurs can't easily accept this loss of direct control where their business is concerned. Most successful businesspeople are hands-on executives who like to make sure details are up to their own exacting standards. And, up to a point, that's a great way to build a successful business. Conversely, it's a lousy way to run a successful franchise program. You must be able to cede day-to-day, detail-intensive control of your franchise outlets to your franchisees (within the rules laid down in your franchise agreement and operations manual, of course).

As owner, you have been able to tell your manager to change the prices, the inventory, the staff, even the tie he's wearing if you don't like it! But, as franchisor, you must suggest, motivate, and persuade rather than command. As an owner, you could fire your manager or other staff members. As a franchisor, it's a different story, because franchisees don't "fire" very easily.

Poor Franchisee Performance

Another potential drawback is the franchisees will be unable to operate the business in the manner that made it successful (and, therefore, franchisable) in the first place.

There are usually two reasons for this occurrence: (1) The franchisee has not been properly trained or is, quite bluntly, incompetent when it comes to this particular business; or (2) the franchisor (as an entrepreneur/business manager) *did* turn out to be indispensable and *no one* (save a cloned replica of the franchisor!) can successfully run this business the same way he or she did. The first case can be, for the most part, avoided by having extensive training and ongoing support programs in place. If that fails, you can retain or eventually (and not without a great deal of hassle) replace the franchisee.

As for the second case, it may be ego-gratifying to find out that you are absolutely irreplaceable when it comes to the success of your business concept, but unless your business can be made (through teaching, development of elaborate manuals, etc.) to run smoothly without your being there, you will have to kiss goodbye your dreams of establishing a successful franchise program. How many businesses fit this description? Not many, but it does happen.

Finding Qualified Franchisees

As the numbers of franchisors has continued to grow, some sources have portrayed the overall situation as a "buyer's market" (as it were) when it comes to finding qualified potential franchisees. On November 14, 1989, *The Wall Street Journal* reported that "small companies looking to expand through franchising say there is a shortage of desirable people who want to buy franchises and that the competition to attract the few good candidates is impossibly tough in the face of established franchisors."

There are hundreds (even thousands) of franchise opportunities available to the potential franchisee, which has led to fierce competition among franchisors to attract the most qualified franchisees. However, the above opinion that it is "impossibly tough" to find good franchisees isn't supported by our experience or the statistics. And here's why:

Statistics show that more than 80 percent of franchise buyers are between the ages of thirty-five and fifty-four. And as the baby boom generation continues to age, the thirty-five–to–fifty-four age group will be the fastest-growing slice of demographics in the United States during the 1990s and beyond. This represents an enormous area of long-term opportunity for franchisors with good, proven concepts and sophisticated marketing techniques.

Also, there are three other solid reasons that the pool of qualified franchisees will continue to grow: (1) continued decentralization or buyouts of large companies, leading to early retirements or layoffs of experienced businesspeople; (2) increasing affluence (even with recession worries, there is always a solid core of people with money and businesses that thrive); and (3) the growing variety of franchise opportunities, many appealing to astute, challenged people with no interest in running hamburger or haircut businesses.

So our considered opinion is *yes*, it can be hard work (in terms of time and money spent) to attract the right franchisees for your program, but the market of potential franchisees is large, and is expected to keep growing, well into the twenty-first century.

Keeping Franchisees—and Keeping Them Happy

Even after you've found qualified and savvy franchisees, they need to be tended and treated fairly, lest they become dissatisfied with your system. It is not unknown for an unhappy franchisee to try to sell a franchise, convert it into a nonfranchised outlet, or attempt to lead a franchisee rebellion against the franchisor. Legal strictures can prevent or at least hamper these efforts, but of course the time to handle problems is early on—by preventing them, if possible. (We will discuss the franchisor-franchisee relationship in more depth in the next chapter.)

Managing Rapid Growth

"How can rapid growth be a disadvantage? Isn't that what we all want out of our franchise programs?" Yes, it is, but don't forget the old adage: Be careful what you wish for, because you might get it. In other words, a program that grows faster than your ability to manage it can be more damaging in terms of cost and reputation than a program that grows slower than you expected.

Case in point: Have you ever heard of D'Lites, a franchise offering low-calorie burgers, salads, and sandwiches? Probably not, though they had a good chance to set the standard for healthy fast food. Born in the early 1980s, just as exercise and health concerns had evolved from a fad into a national obsession, D'Lites looked like a sure winner. In its first four years, D'Lites opened a respectable eighty-six restaurants, nearly three-quarters of those sold to franchisees. Its founder had dreams of D'Lites becoming a one-thousand-outlet chain in less than a decade.

But the go-go attitude that fostered the quick initial sales (and that grandiose dream) was not backed up with franchisee support or savvy market analysis. When mainstream fast-food outlets responded to the challenge of a more health-conscious clientele by adding lighter fare such as salads and chicken to their menus, D'Lites failed to capitalize on its established base and still-strong point of difference. This period also saw internal financial strife in the chain, as corporate money that was desperately needed to promote the suddenly struggling chain was apparently being spent to buy out floundering franchises belonging to D'Lites corporate executives. Morale sunk and losses grew. By the time the decade was over, rather than boasting one-thousand-plus outlets, D'Lites had all but disappeared.

Taken together, these disadvantages can seem a little daunting. But, remember, the above was just a shopping list of major things that *can* go wrong with a franchise program. Armed with knowledge about these pitfalls, you are better equipped to avoid them. Forewarned is forearmed.

Which Businesses Make Good Franchises—and Why?

In Chapter 1, while examining the downside to franchising, we cited some examples of characteristics of businesses that were *not* prime candidates for franchising. Conversely, we will now take a look at what kinds of business have the best chance at success as franchises—and why.

Businesses That Are Easily Replicated and Easily Run

ServiceMaster—the home- and office-cleaning franchise—has quietly become a major success story (doing $1 billion in sales annually, with approximately four thousand franchised outlets). One of the major factors that led to its strong showing is that it's an easy business to get into—supplies, equipment, and training are provided—and it's an easy business to run. No allowances have to be made for the tastes or needs of different regions; no elaborate tasks have to be learned. The franchisees just clean, helping ServiceMaster to "clean up" (as it were) in its field.

On the other hand, businesses that are *too* simple are sometimes too easily copied. A franchisor still needs a system that gives its franchisees distinct and real advantages. Conversely, complex businesses such as real estate, business consulting, and hotels *can* be successfully franchised, but we're talking here about general traits of the *most easily franchisable* types of businesses.

Businesses with New Ideas or a New Twist in a Proven Market

Ice cream shops, led by first Dairy Queen and Tastee-Freez, and later by Baskin-Robbins and Bresler's, are well established, but somewhat old-hat. Surprisingly, the 1980s saw tremendous growth in a new category of dessert-oriented shops: those selling frozen yogurt. With The Country's Best Yogurt (TCBY) leading the way, frozen yogurt shops have multiplied from a handful to more than 2,500 outlets in less than a decade. In response, most ice cream chains (and even McDonald's) have added frozen yogurt to their menus. Just when it looked like the ice cream segment of franchising was "frozen," a new idea shook things up.

Businesses Whose Concepts Are Broad Enough to Fit Their Market Aims

There's nothing wrong with being solely a local success, if that's all you aspire to be. But to achieve national prominence, you may find that your concept needs refining or broadening. If your business wouldn't necessarily appeal to audiences outside of your home market, you may find yourself hamstrung when you try to expand.

An example of this is barbecue—a popular style of cooking food that is not represented by a nationally successful chain. A main reason for this is that authentic barbecue is, for the most part, a matter of regional taste. Some areas of the country favor beef over pork; others prefer hot sauce to sweet sauce. These preferences are so strong as to preclude (thus far) a single barbecue chain from gaining prominence.

Recently there have been a couple of new entrants who may change that by offering a product whose taste is distinctive but broadly appealing enough to transcend most regional prejudices. Even so, they may have a tough time in pockets of the South and West where the prevailing attitude is, "If it ain't our kind of barbecue, it ain't barbecue!" The moral is: If you want to have a regional chain, a regional idea is fine, however, if you desire a franchise that is national in scope and penetration, you need an idea and a business system that works as well in Manhattan, New York, as it does in Manhattan, Kansas.

Businesses That Are Not Personality-, Site-, or Fad-Specific

A good example of this type of business is Merle Harmon's Fan Fair shops, founded by local Milwaukee and Texas sports broadcaster Merle Harmon. A contributing factor to Fan Fair's success is it *doesn't* depend on Harmon personally or a fixed set of sports teams—instead it offers gifts and clothing featuring the logos and colors of dozens of the most popular professional and collegiate sports teams. While the popularity of these teams can vary with their win-loss records, Fan Fair covers all the bases (so to speak) by stocking the memorabilia of a wide variety of teams.

On the other hand, the last few years have seen a proliferation of celebrity restaurants and/or bars. And while some of these do quite well on reputation alone (especially in New York and Los Angeles, where the celebrities involved are merely investors or once-a-month show-ups), others, especially in smaller markets or those built around sports celebrities, simply *must* have the celebrity on site a reasonable amount of the time to draw customers. Obviously, these types of establishments are *not* good candidates for franchising. The same goes for businesses whose unique locations (such as a restaurant overlooking a waterfall) are not easily duplicated.

While these are good examples of *types* of businesses that are promising candidates for franchising, lets break the process down even further and identify individual *traits* we believe help strongly indicate the readiness of a business for the challenge of franchising.

Nine Keys to Franchisability

As with other measurable qualities, the franchisability of a business can be determined at least in general terms by comparing the characteristics of that business against a set of established conditions. While these nine keys to franchisability are not the be-all and end-all of predicting whether a business has the potential for success as a franchise, they can provide a clearer understanding of what it takes to establish a solid and eventually prosperous franchise program. (As always, the marketplace has the final say—and, as we suggest throughout this book, the advice of franchising experts should be sought and heeded.)

Size

Is your business large enough to convey an image of success to potential franchisees? Of course, your business need not be General Motors or Exxon to accomplish this—many smaller operators have made excellent franchisors—but it should compare favorably to others in your field. Franchisees are, in fact, investing in you and your dream, and the bigger and therefore more successful your dream looks, the more impressive—and, perhaps, most importantly, the more *reassuring*—it will be to them.

Longevity

Has your business been in operation long enough to have reached a solid level of success? Are those day-to-day operational flaws that crop up in any business becoming much fewer and farther between? Can you confidently predict its levels of sales and market share in the immediate and long-term future? There's a great deal to be said for new businesses—in fact, the majority of current franchises were started since 1980—but your business must be sufficiently established to demonstrate that it is functionally sound and has a bright future.

Profitability

Bluntly put, is your business making money? If not, you're looking in the wrong direction. A franchise program is a way to make an established business grow, *not* a way to try to put a struggling business in the black. If *you* aren't making money with your system, how can you expect franchisees to turn a profit?

Make no mistake, if your franchisees aren't successful, you won't be either.

Teachability

Can other people be taught to run your business in the same way you do, the way that has made it successful? For example, do you or your senior staff (whichever is best applicable) have an easy or difficult time training managers and/or general employees? Franchising a business is, in effect, teaching that business to other people, over and over—particularly to those who may have little or no experience in your field. The easier it is to impart your way of doing business to others, the better your chances of success in the long run. (This does not mean that your business cannot be complicated. However, if your business has a more complex concept, you may be best off looking for franchisees with a high degree of experience and/or expertise in your field, or at least allowing for a long training program. Many full-service restaurants, for instance, train their franchisees for more than a month.)

System Replication

Tied to the teachability of your concept is whether its inherent tasks and duties can be fully analyzed and clearly described. Your franchisees will not be able to rely on your years of knowledge every moment of every day—they will instead turn to a detailed operations manual for assistance. The two key questions are: (1) Can every facet of your operation be boiled down to understandable written and/or illustrated instructions? and (2) Can these instructions be followed without the background knowledge about the business that you have to a successful end?

Marketability

You know that your pizzas or accounting services or sports apparel can be successfully marketed—that's how your business has grown to the level it's already reached. But what you need to know is, can your *business system* be effectively communicated and sold to others? And these "others" are more than consumers;

they're both consumers *and* potential businesspeople. They are looking, in effect, to invest in a business *and* in themselves. Perhaps they will choose your business, but only if you can convincingly relate the strengths of your business to them. That is much more challenging than selling someone a pizza or a new muffler.

Transferability

How universal is your business? Is your product or service local or national in scope? Will it work in different markets? Will it work in different economic or cultural segments of your own market? While at first it's a good idea to expand in your own area, to become fully successful you must eventually penetrate other markets, and that will work only if your business can adapt to the perhaps differing needs of those markets.

Originality

For your best shot at success (all other things being equal), your business needs a point of difference from your competitors. You can have the same basic product or service as "the other guys," but your chances of success will improve by offering a difference in price, delivery/presentation, quality, or quantity. Call it your Unique Selling Proposition (USP)—it's what makes you!

We mentioned a good example of this before: the difficulty Domino's Pizza had in initially penetrating the Chicago-area market, where local mini-chains and neighborhood independent pizzerias are well established. If Domino's were just another pizza chain, it might well have failed in this important and lucrative market. But its USP was speedy delivery and fairly low cost, and these differences gave it a unique foothold that has allowed it to survive in a very competitive market. A related important point to consider is this: An original idea in your market may be old hat in another market. For example, *your* market may eat up (pardon the pun) your restaurant's cheesesteak sandwiches, but just try and import those sandwiches to Philadelphia (where, of course, the cheesesteak is king and its local purveyors are well established). The effort would be doomed to fail.

Affordability

As we said above, in Key 3, your business must be profitable, but it also must be potentially profitable for your franchisees. How do these points differ? Remember that your franchisee's profit comes after paying for the initial investment in the business, including your franchise fee and all of the costs of starting the business—not to mention the ongoing royalty they will be paying you. An unrealistically high fee and royalty may fill your pockets at first, but if franchisees are eventually bled dry by those and other expenses, you'll find your sources of income drying up just as fast. In other words, there must be a margin of profit for both you and your franchisees. A corollary to this point is the fact that very expensive startups don't *necessarily* preclude sales—multimillion-dollar costs are common for franchised hotels, for example—but they *do* limit the pool of prospects.

Test the Franchisability of Your Business

Now that you have a better idea of what it takes for a business to be franchisable, we're going to put *your* business to the test!

The following yes-or-no questions have been designed to reward businesses with (relative) strengths in the important and quantifiable categories we examined above. Of course, we *can't* test for intangibles—those "unknown quantities" that can make one business flourish while another similar business flops. And we can't guarantee results; a business that scores high may collapse under the weight of inept, unprepared, or merely unlucky management. Conversely, a low-scoring business can overcome its potential drawbacks through hard work, innovative ideas, and resourceful management.

For each question below, answer yes or no. Answer *all* of the questions, paying close attention to the wording of the questions (since some are similar). While this test is not meant to be a replacement for a thorough and professional analysis of your company's past, present, and future by a qualified franchise consulting firm (such as Don's company, Francorp), it *can* give you a general idea on whether (or how soon) franchising should become part of your business-expansion strategy.

Remember, to accurately gauge your business' franchisability, you must answer yes or no to *all* of the following questions. Here we go!

1. Has your business been in operation for more than a year?   **YES** ___ **NO** ___

2. Has your business been in operation for more than three years?   **YES** ___ **NO** ___

3. Is your business currently profitable?   **YES** ___ **NO** ___

4. Do you have more than one outlet in operation?   **YES** ___ **NO** ___

5. Do you have more than three outlets in operation?   **YES** ___ **NO** ___

6. Do you have more than five outlets in operation?   **YES** ___ **NO** ___

7. Have people asked about the possibility of buying a franchise of your business?   **YES** ___ **NO** ___

8. Do you average three or more inquiries per month about buying a franchise?   **YES** ___ **NO** ___

9. Could you teach the right person how to operate your business in six weeks or less?   **YES** ___ **NO** ___

10. Could you teach the right person how to operate your business in four weeks or less?   **YES** ___ **NO** ___

11. Could you teach the right person how to operate your business in two weeks or less?   YES ___ NO ___

12. Can you confidently leave someone else in charge of your current outlet(s) for a period of time?   YES ___ NO ___

13. Do you operate under a distinctive name, trademark, and/or logo?   YES ___ NO ___

14. Do you have clear criteria for determining a good location for a new outlet?   YES ___ NO ___

15. Do you have sufficient staff so that you or someone else can take a reasonable portion of his or her time away from daily operations and devote that time to your franchise program?   YES ___ NO ___

16. Does your business have a "point of difference" that clearly distinguishes it from competitors?   YES ___ NO ___

17. Do you have $50,000 or more available to develop your franchise program?   YES ___ NO ___

18. Do you have $100,000 or more available to develop your franchise program?   YES ___ NO ___

19. Do you have $200,000 or more available to develop your franchise program?   YES ___ NO ___

20. Do you have three or more years of management experience?   YES ___ NO ___

21. Do you have five or more years of management experience?   YES ___ NO ___

22. Do you have seven or more years of management experience?   YES ___ NO ___

23. Would a franchise need *less* than $400,000 in cash (besides the financeable portion) to open one of your outlets?   YES ___ NO ___

24. Would a franchisee need *less* than $200,000 in cash (besides the financeable portion) to open one of your units?   YES ___ NO ___

25. Would a franchisee need *less* than $100,000 in cash (besides the financeable portion) to open one of your units?   YES ___ NO ___

Scoring

Give yourself 4 points for each "yes" answer. Then compare your score with the following ratings.

0–16: Not Ready. While your business (in its present state) may be sound, important factors indicate it's far from ready for franchising. More seasoning, refining, and research are needed before you should even consider entering the field. An early wrong decision could cost you plenty in terms of time, money, and reputation.

20–36: Slowly Building. Your business fits some of the *minimum* criteria for franchising, but is still weak in some other areas. Identifying those areas and working to rectify them can improve your chances for future success in franchising.

40–52: Getting Closer. A good future candidate. You have likely been in business long enough to identify and correct your general trouble spots. It may be a bit premature to attempt to launch a franchise program, but some further work in the direction you are already headed could speed things up. Seek franchise consulting help to identify, assess, and assist in improving your weak areas.

54–76: A Solid Contender. All the signs seem promising. You should take a very serious look at franchising as a means of expanding your business. Seek franchise consulting help to set up a development plan and schedule for an optional franchise strategy.

80–100: Poised for Success. Your business has outstanding potential for rapid growth and market domination through franchising. If your assessment is accurate, you have a proven business concept, a broad and waiting market, and sufficient capital to make it happen. Seek franchise consulting help immediately to make a smooth transition from a thriving business to a thriving franchisor.

Would You Make a Good Franchisor?

If you have been completely fair and honest (perhaps brutally so) in evaluating your business, you should now have a clearer idea of its franchisability. And while this is the most important part of deciding whether to franchise, it is not the *only* important part. You must also take an unbiased look at how you would fare *personally* as a franchisor.

No matter whether you currently describe yourself as an entrepreneur, a manager, an executive, or a plain old regular *boss*, as a franchisor you will be something different. Rest assured, the skills you employed to build your business will also come in handy as you build your franchise program, but you will also need other skills. In fact, many successful businesspeople find that creating successful franchise programs can be an even greater challenge than creating the original businesses that spawned these programs!

The following list of personality characteristics is not meant to sound preachy or overly simplistic; the simple fact is that being a franchisor requires a sometimes gentler and more diplomatic touch than many entrepreneurs are used to employing. A good franchisor must have patience, trust, flexibility, and strong communication skills.

Patience

Realize your franchisees are not *you*. If they were like you—if they had the same backgrounds and dreams you have—they might be your competitors rather than your franchisees. You need to be patient with their approach to and grasp of your concept. With steady nurturing and continuing support, you can grow a crop of successful franchisees in your image, but with the added diversity of their *own* personality strengths.

Trust

We don't mean to imply that successful businesspeople generally lack confidence in their employees or associates. However, as a franchisor, you will quite literally put the success of your program in someone else's hands—the hands of your franchisees. You must trust them implicitly. It sounds like a cliché to say that you're all in it together, but you are. Their success will be your success, so there must be reciprocal trust.

Flexibility

Franchisees are *not* employees. But they are not quite partners, either. They are a special hybrid and as such require special handling. You can't fire franchisees, you have to work with them to iron out disputes. You *do* have considerable power because of your position and the strength of a franchise contract. But remember, not every disagreement is a fight. You need to be flexible enough to allow your franchisees to contribute their ideas. (Remember the Big Mac!)

Communication

Simply put, you must be able to talk and listen to your franchisees. You can't just talk *at* them (telling them what you want them to do), nor can you be biased, listening only to those aspects of their complaints *you* feel are most important. True communication and dialogue are important keys to the ongoing success of a franchise relationship. If you need to implement a change in the system, you have to be able to clearly tell your franchisees *why* you are making this change. And, since they are the ones who are "out there," representing you to the public, you need to listen carefully and thoughtfully to their concerns. The future of your program may depend upon their hearing you and your hearing them clearly.

These characteristics may sound a bit "touchy-feely" to you, and perhaps they are. But the fact remains that being a franchisor requires a deft and sometimes delicate touch. Brush up your diplomacy!

Something New

We've helped you evaluate both your business *and* yourself. But there's one last question to ask yourself: Are you ready to learn a new business?

Because that's what franchising is—its own business, as USA Baby's Al Levine said in the last chapter. Franchising has its own set of rules, regulations, customs, joys, and headaches. You may be a great copy-shop owner or a terrific chicken restaurant manager, but now you are poised to become something different—something new, with which you have no experience. You can still consider yourself an entrepreneur or a business owner or whatever else you'd like to call yourself, but realize if you are running a franchise program, you will be, first and foremost, a franchisor.

That may sound obvious, but it is true that you are embarking on a completely new path, one that may ultimately take you farther than you could have ever previously progressed. It's time to learn new rules and how to apply them. It's time to gather all the advice you can from experts in the field, and use it to create your own operating philosophy. In short, it's time for an exciting new challenge. And if you're like most successful businesspeople the prospect of a *new challenge* may entice you far beyond any dreams of mere riches!

The Next Step

Where to go from here? First, some congratulations are in order.

By taking an analytical, point-by-point look at your business and yourself—from perspectives you may have never considered —you are positioned to make better-informed decisions about the future of your company, whether you choose to franchise or not. We know that this sort of intense mirror-gazing isn't easy, but we think you'll agree that it is worth it in the long run. Remember: Knowledge begins with understanding yourself. And, if you have decided that both you *and* your business are ready for franchising, you're reading for the next step.

Turn the page and begin the next chapter, which will tell you *how* to go about franchising your business.

Chapter Eight

Becoming a Franchisor, Part II: How to Franchise Your Business

At this point in your examination of franchising as a method to further expand your business, you have reached an important crossroads. By now, you should have a balanced picture of franchising and what it can do for qualified and prepared businesses. And after examining both the advantages and disadvantages of franchising as a business-expansion vehicle, you may have concluded franchising offers greater potential for sustained growth than other means of expansion. But it is one thing to arrive at that conclusion and quite another to take the steps needed to become a franchisor. In this case you must not only do the right thing, but you must do it right!

This, then, is the mission of this particular chapter: to

demonstrate and explain options and requirements in these four areas: (1) Strategic planning; (2) creation of materials and marketing; (3) sales/awarding; and (4) initial followup—vital stages in the development of a successful franchise program.

In other words, if you choose that branch of the crossroads marked "franchising," here's your map.

The Use of Consultants

Before we start with the four major sections of this chapter, we'd like to give you some advice. Launching a franchise program for your business can involve complexities that suggest the need for *qualified* and *experienced* assistance. Just as you readily consult a lawyer with legal questions, and a banker or accountant for financial questions, it may make sense to go to a franchise consultant for professional advice and assistance in this complex field.

The International Franchise Association (IFA), located in Washington, D.C., can provide a list of consulting businesses that offer franchise development services. When checking into the backgrounds and services of these consulting companies, look for those with proven track records of assisting successful franchisors. Visit their places of business, and review samples of their work for other clients. Make sure that they have staff that can handle all aspects of your program. Also, get a list of at least ten franchisor clients of the firms you are investigating—and then call them and ask *their* opinion of the consulting firm. Armed with this knowledge, you are more likely to find a firm that matches your needs.

Strategic Growth Planning

What we call strategic growth planning really consists of decision making. And, as you can well imagine, *many* decisions need to be made before you establish your franchise program, such as: Is franchising the answer to your expansion needs? If so, just what kind of program should you offer? What kind of franchises will you sell? How much will they cost? What will the term of the contract be? What will you call your franchise company and outlets? (You probably didn't think of that question, but the name you currently use may be unusable or undesirable in the long run; we will cover this in more depth later on.)

The strategic planning part of developing your program will include many elements, but among the most important will be research, selecting franchise types, setting fees and royalties, determining franchise territories, setting the term of the agreement, and dealing with trademarks and logos.

Research

Before intelligent decisions can be made concerning the form of your franchise program, it can be useful to examine the structure of other franchise programs—especially those of your direct competitors (if any). At the very least, you will want to know these things: What investment (cash plus noncash) is being required of the franchisees? What services are being provided by the franchisor? What franchise fees, royalties, and advertising fees are being assessed? What other payments or purchases are required? What kinds of franchisees are they attracting? How is the territory defined? What is the duration of the franchise agreement?

The books previously referred to in Chapter 4 (most notably, *The Sourcebook of Franchise Opportunities*) will list most—though not all—of your competitors and will provide you with some of this information. However, for a more detailed review of your competitors, you should obtain the offering circulars of these franchisors. (Offering circulars are comprehensive documents that describe a franchise program; they will be more fully discussed in Chapter 9.)

With knowledge gleaned from these documents, you can get a feel for the yardsticks of franchising that are common in your particular industry. This may sound easy, but this process entails a great deal of research—and much of it requires knowing where to look for such information as well as properly assessing it. In this case, it's what you don't know that can be disastrous. This underscores our suggestion about using a qualified franchise consulting firm; there is no reason to reinvent the wheel.

Franchise Types

The next step is to determine the type (or types) of franchises you are going to offer. There are four to be considered, although, by no means, are all four "right" for all businesses: (1) individual franchises, (2) multiunit or area development franchises, (3) subfranchises, and (4) conversion franchises. The question every new franchisor must ask is, Which one (or combination, in some cases) of these options should I offer to prospective franchisees? The answer to that question will depend upon both the characteristics of the franchisor's business and the franchisor's goals. Let's look at each type in more detail.

Individual Franchises

These are awarded to an individual, group of individuals, or a company for one business unit to be operated at one location or one geographically defined area.

In most cases, especially in the early stages of a franchise program, offering individual franchises is the easiest, most cost-effective, and least risky option. For one thing, buyers for individual units are likely to be easier to find and, once found, easier to deal with than the usually more sophisticated multiunit buyer. Then, too, the franchisor must also undergo a "learning curve" period as he or she finds out firsthand about the realities of franchise relationships; it is generally better to keep things as simple as possible until that learning period is over.

Multiunit or Area Development Franchises

This type of franchise is awarded to an individual, group, or company for a territory in which more than one unit will be established and operated by the franchisee.

173

Unquestionably, the sale of multiple units to a franchisee *who is ready to open them immediately* is the most rapid means of franchise expansion. But for a company new to franchising, it can be difficult to attract buyers capable of the large cash outlay it takes to open multiple units.

Moreover, multiunit development can actually be *slower* than growth by individual units if the units in the multiunit territories are *not* developed simultaneously. In practice, multiunit buyers often are not capable of opening all of their units at once or simply do not choose to do so, preferring instead to test the waters with one, then gradually adding the additional units. In contrast, you might well find that by instead of offering *individual franchises* in the territory, you can more quickly attract separate buyers for the full number of other units the territory could support.

To avoid this potential problem of "wait and see" where territory development is concerned, we strongly recommend any franchisor require multiunit buyers to adhere to a performance schedule requiring that a certain number of units be developed within a certain time frame. This can help franchisors sidestep a situation that even many big-league franchisors (such as McDonald's) have encountered—having to buy back from a balky franchisee (usually at a premium price) a lucrative territory that is being developed too slowly or not at all.

Subfranchises

In this system, subfranchises are awarded to an individual, group, or company for a territory in which several individual franchises will be sold, usually by the subfranchisor, and usually operated under the subfranchisor's administration and supervision.

The subfranchisor normally does not operate units, other than a single "showcase" unit with headquarters and training facilities. Instead, the subfranchisor takes a large burden from the franchisor's shoulders by selling individual and/or multiunit franchises within his or her territory, often training the franchisees and making periodic supervisory visits. In return, the subfranchisor customarily shares in both the franchise fee and royalty paid by the franchisee(s), usually taking a larger portion than the franchisor.

Many large franchisors—among them Century 21 and Budget Rent A Car—have used subfranchising to successfully accelerate growth, especially during highly competitive periods when becoming established in new markets as quickly as possible was of critical importance. However, this form of franchising should not be undertaken lightly. For example, franchisors who are quality-control sensitive may not want to give up critical responsibilities to a third party. And there is always the consideration that the franchisor gives up substantial income in return for the sub's services.

Conversion Franchises

We covered this type of franchising in depth in Chapter 2; briefly, it consists of converting existing independent businesses into franchised outlets. Conversion franchising works most effectively in industries with scattered, established independent entities (such as real estate, construction/home improvement, and hotel/motels), and in industries where the advantages of belonging to a group (such as the power of cooperative advertising or buying) are more critical than the actual techniques of running the individual businesses. Century 21 is perhaps the best-known leading conversion franchisor.

Setting Fees and Royalties

Franchise fees and royalties are the two basic income sources for most franchise programs. This initial, one-time franchise fee enables the franchisor to recover to some degree, if not completely, the costs involved in developing the franchise program, selling the franchise, training the franchisee, and providing support for new franchisees during the start-up period when expenses to the franchisor will likely exceed the royalty income received.

What should your franchise fee be? At least three factors should be considered: (1) What competitors in your industry and your investment range charge, (2) the franchisee's return on investment (R.O.I.) and (3) your total cost to start the franchisee in business (plus a profit). Obviously, these factors will vary from franchise to franchise, but there is a fine line that must be walked: The fee must be low enough so the franchisees have little difficulty paying it (after all, they are likely to be making a large, total investment in the franchise, of which the initial fee is only part), and yet the fee must be high enough to enable the franchisor to provide the initial services and support the franchisee will require.

This last factor is equally important—perhaps even more so—in regard to setting the right royalty percentage, since the royalty will be collected for the length of the franchise agreement. Royalties vary from industry to industry, but, generally, the more services the franchisor has to provide, the higher the royalty should be to cover the costs of these services while still leaving margin for franchisor profit. The franchisee's volume and margin also play a role in determining royalty rates. In restaurants and specialty retail stores, for example, royalties usually average from 4 to 6 percent (with rates often a point or two lower for franchisors whose units generate particularly high sales volumes). Royalties for service businesses are typically 8 to 10 percent (although we have seen them go as high as 20 percent, especially for businesses with low volumes).

Royalties are usually paid as a percentage of sales, or sometimes as a minimum fee against a percentage of sales; in almost no cases should royalties be a fixed dollar amount. Royalties should be collected at least weekly; franchisors who collect royalties monthly are really making their franchisees a loan of this money. And especially in the early stages of your program, this is a form of beneficence that you can ill afford. Joe likes to tell the story about a franchisee who questioned the franchisor as to why the royalty was collected weekly. The response is a classic: "I'd prefer to collect them hourly, but it's too much work. So, I guess I'll have to collect them weekly." Prompt collection of royalties can also alert a franchisor if a franchise starts doing poorly in sales in relation to past performance or to other similar outlets, so he or she can correct problems before they get dangerous.

To encourage sales of multiple units, you may wish to offer incentive, such as splitting the total franchise fee into payments of half down and the remainder as each of the units open. You may also wish to fractionally decrease fees and/or royalties as a multiunit franchisee opens a certain number of units. Or if you are selling a subfranchise territory, you can charge a certain amount for rights to the market, and then take a small portion of the franchise fee collected by the subfranchisor and perhaps one-third of the monies he or she collects as royalties. These relationships and ranges (using a hypothetical franchise with an individual fee of $35,000 and royalty rate of 6 percent) are illustrated in the chart below.

Type of franchise	Franchise fees earned by franchisor	Royalties earned by franchisor
Individual	$35,000	6 percent
Multiunit (10 units)	$25,000 each, payable as $125,000 down, $12,500 as each unit opens	6 percent (1–3 units); 5.75 percent (after 3); 5.5 percent (after 5); 5.25 percent (after 7); 5 percent (when all 10 open)
Subfranchise	$100,000 for territory plus $2,500 per unit sold	2 percent (⅓ of the 6 percent collected by the subfranchisor)

Fees and royalties for conversion franchises vary, but because newly converted franchises usually start with an established base of existing business that the franchisee is likely to be reluctant to pay a royalty on, the franchise fee is usually lower (maybe one-half the price of a normal individual franchise); the royalty sometimes begins at a reduced rate that grows to the franchisor's nonconversion rate after a few years. For example, the rate may start at 1 percent the first year and increase by a percentage point or two each year until it reaches the full rate after three, four, or five years. Or the royalty can be determined by using the franchisee's previous year's sales (as an independent entity) as a ceiling and charging the regular royalty on any sales above that amount. In general, since you're dealing with experienced businesspeople and are trying to convince them to join your system, you should be ready to apply creative methods to create a mutually agreeable (*and* mutually profitable) arrangement.

A final note: Calculation of royalties, while an art not a science, should be done with care based on the need for a "win-win" situation long term. Before you make a final decision you should run pro formas and do sensitivity analysis at different percentages and different possible levels of sales volume. Remember that both you and your franchisees will have to live with this decision for a long time.

Determining Franchise Territories

By "territories" we mean a geographic area in which no other franchise company-owned unit will be situated or will otherwise conduct business. The two related questions each franchisor must answer regarding territories are (1) how large should they be? and (2) on what criteria should the size be based?

Criteria can vary widely, depending on the type of business and especially on the type of customers the business caters to. For example, looking at population alone may be sufficient to determine the territory for a fast-food franchise, but for a business-service franchise, the number of businesses in a given area would be a more important factor. And even after the *criteria* for size have been determined, it still may not be easy to pinpoint the size itself. You have to follow a Goldilocks strategy: it can't be too small (unhappy franchisees) or too large (lost sales opportunities: unhappy franchisor); it must be "just right." What is "just right" in your case? One way of approaching that question is to ask another: What's the smallest size the territory must be to give the franchisee sufficient customers to be profitable or to meet the desired return R.O.I.? You can begin to answer this question with some accuracy if you have an existing business by determining the geographical makeup of your present customer base, perhaps through a survey. If you discover, for example, that three-quarters of the customers of your average outlet live and/or work within a two-mile radius of the outlet and the residential and business population for that two-mile area is around twenty-five thousand people, you might decide to set your territory size at an approximately two-mile radius containing twenty thousand to thirty thousand people.

Of course, you've undoubtedly encountered McDonald's restaurants (or outlets of other "superstar" franchises) within blocks of each other, especially in big cities or other densely populated areas (such as college towns). McDonald's, in fact, grants no territories; the franchise is for the street address of the outlet only. But you must remember this is the policy of a thirty-five-plus-year-old franchise program with more than 12,000 outlets worldwide . . . In the early days of *your* program, you should worry more about selling than about saturation!

Setting the Term of Agreement

You must have a formal agreement with your franchise (covered in detail in Chapter 9), but how long should that agreement be in effect? Five years? Twenty years? Forever?

Back in the early days of franchising, franchisors didn't always answer that question intelligently. Tastee-Freez, then a fast-growing chain of ice cream stores, once granted a sixty-six-county territory to a franchisee without a performance schedule and with no limit to the duration of the agreement. After twenty years, only nine units were in operation in the territory. The franchisee had died and his widow had no desire to open additional units. Tastee-Freez was left with two relatively unattractive options: (1) Buy back the territory at a (presumably high) price named by the franchisee's widow, or (2) allow the lucrative territory to remain underdeveloped and lose millions in potential revenue. Such excruciating decisions can be avoided by establishing a reasonable term of agreement (and, as we stated above, a performance schedule for large territories).

What should be the duration of the term? The two most important factors to consider are the size of investment and the term of the unit's lease.

Size of Investment

The larger the franchisee's investment, the longer the franchisee will need to recoup it. For example, the term of agreement for a hotel franchise might be twenty-five years, while that for an ice cream outlet might only be five years. Obviously, the buyer of a hotel franchise is going to lay out and/or borrow much more money than would the buyer of an ice cream store. Franchisees and franchisors both need to have a reasonable return on their investments—a rate higher than could be obtained by leaving their money in a safe investment, like a Treasury bond (as we covered in Chapter 5).

Term of the Unit's Lease

Sometimes, particularly in enclosed malls, the term of agreement is tied to the length of the unit's lease. When the lease ends, the agreement ends (since continuation of the lease is integral to the continued success of that particular unit).

In general, we recommend five- to ten-year initial terms (depending on the size of the investment), with two or three automatic five-year renewals at the franchisee's option, subject to the franchisee remaining in compliance with the agreement and signing the then-current agreement at the then-current terms. This gives you, the franchisor, the option and opportunity to revise royalties or other aspects of the agreement periodically. It also gives you the option to convert territories to company ownership in fifteen or twenty years if you want to at that time.

It should be noted, however, that many states have enacted franchise "relationship" laws which require *mandatory* renewal of the relationship at the franchisee's option as long as they have substantially complied with the terms and conditions of the franchise agreement. In effect, then, many franchisees have been granted terms in perpetuity. In the light of these perhaps meddling laws, the main reason many franchisors now put a distinct length of term into franchise agreements is to force the franchise to upgrade its outlet to the current standards as a condition and/or adjust the terms periodically. (Of course, a franchisee who is in violation of the agreement can be terminated at any time—usually, however, not without a fight. This will be covered in depth in Chapter 9, which focuses on legal topics.)

Dealing with Trademarks and Logos

Not every franchisable business is blessed with a protectable or desirable name. The name of your business may be too nonspecific to protect it (such as Quick Food or Color Copying) or may conflict with a business name that is already a federally registered trademark. As you may well imagine, any of you out there named McDonald (or even MacDonald) can forget about naming your business after yourself if you sell hamburgers—or even if you are in some other business that McDonald's trademark attorneys might consider "confusingly similar" to the public. For example, there is a wonderfully colorful and convoluted fight now in process in New York City over the name Ray's Pizza (and various permutations thereof). This fight began as the legend grew among New York insiders that the best pizza in the city could be found at a pizza parlor named Ray's. But is this ambrosial delight available at Ray's or at Famous Ray's? Or perhaps at Ray's House of Pizza, Ray's Pizza, or Ray's Real Pizza? Other contenders include Ray's Famous Pizza and Ray's Famous Pizza of Greenwich Village (which are separate and individual entities), and Original Ray's and Original Ray's Pizza (ditto). There are over twenty outlets of one version or another of Ray's in Manhattan and they are likely to spend a lot of money on lawyers in an attempt to untangle the mess (we suspect the eventual winner of this battle will want to holler "hoo-RAY!"). This is an obvious case where an ounce of prevention (in the form of registering a name) can be worth a pound of pizza.

The purpose of obtaining a federally registered trademark, of course, is to restrict anyone else throughout the United States from doing business under that name and with that trademark. To be protected nationally, your mark must be registered with the U.S. Patent and Trademark Office, although there are reasons why you may wish to have your mark registered in certain states as well. (One is that after applying for a federal trademark you can expect to wait a year or longer for approval; state registrations are quicker and enable you to establish a record for doing business under that name on a given date, which can be helpful if a dispute should arise.)

When seeking to obtain a registered trademark, it is mandatory to consult an attorney who specializes in trademark law. This attorney will undertake a trademark search to determine whether your name might be the same as (or confusingly similar to) other registered trademarks already in use elsewhere in the country, and advise you whether the name is too generic. For instance, Joe is the founder of the Chief Executive Officers Clubs, a nonprofit association of CEO's running businesses (the average sales of which is about $20 million). Joe sought to trademark the name Chief Executive Officer or CEO. His attorney advised that would be difficult to defend because it is generic. Just as you can't trademark a name like The Shoe Store or The Phone Company, it's almost impossible to trademark something already in common usage like the term Chief Executive Officer. What Joe *could* and *did* trademark, however, was the mark or logo for the Chief Executive Officers Clubs:

Consequently no one can use this mark without violating the trademark of the CEO Clubs.

The name is just one of several ingredients that blend

together to professionalize your public image. Another very important image enhancer is a business's logo (the stylized lettering or design that's used in conjunction with the business's name). A good one will convey at a glance what your business is about and can help attract the kind of customer you desire. A bad one will reflect mediocrity, no matter how excellent all other aspects of your business may be. Few expenditures you make in the course of your business development will have the lasting value of the dollars you pay a skilled professional designer to create a logo that is accomplished-looking and conveys the image that is appropriate to your particular business. As usual, our advice is to get it done right by going to professionals.

With this extensive strategic planning complete, you can begin to assemble the marketing and operations materials needed to back up a franchise program.

Marketing and Operational Materials

As with most business undertakings, developing a franchise program requires the development of a particular set of documents and materials. These materials generally fall into three categories: (1) operations (and the operations manual), (2) marketing, and (3) legal. We will cover perhaps the most important of these, the operations manual, here; we cover marketing materials in a following subsection. The principal legal documents needed by a franchisors are discussed at length in Chapter 9.

The Operations Manual

The cornerstone of your franchise program will be your operations manual. If you have built a successful business, you've made mistakes along the way that have probably cost you money. Of course, you don't want your franchisees to repeat those mistakes—you want them to replicate your hard-earned success from their very first day in business. When they win, you win.

To ensure they adopt your business system and adhere to it,

you should describe clearly and in detail how that system operates from the moment the business opens each day until it closes each night. That is the function of the operations manual. It also should be cross-referenced to the franchise agreement, so that its provisions and procedures have the force of contractual obligation.

In theory, a good operations manual is so thorough it eliminate the need for phone calls to clarify how and when to do something. Typical franchise operations manuals are divided into sections for easy reference, and are often held together in some looseleaf manner to easily allow additions and deletions as they become necessary. We don't recommend printing it as a final, be-all and end-all book, because, by its definition, it should be a dynamic and changing source of information.

Sample sections including the following:

Introduction

The introduction sets the tone for the manual. It often includes a message from the president or chairman of the company, as well as a basic company philosophy. This is a great place for a clear and concise mission statement. This section should describe the franchise program, list the services the franchisee can expect from your organization, and identify the primary responsibilities of the franchisee.

Preopening Procedures

This section of the manual covers all of the steps a franchisee must take prior to opening, including (as appropriate and/or necessary) locating and securing a site, purchasing equipment and supplies, acquiring licenses and permits, opening bank accounts, and preparing for the grand opening.

Personnel

This section covers hiring and dealing with employees, including placing ads and conducting interviews, keeping employee records, scheduling shifts, reviewing employees, and firing employees.

Coverage should be devoted to both management employees and sales/labor staffs.

Administrative Procedures

Here you introduce your franchisees to the style of management needed to successfully operate your franchises. The section should detail administrative tasks such as billing and collections, purchasing inventory and record keeping, as well as provide standardized guidelines for controlling costs, reporting sales, and generating a profit.

Daily Operational Procedures

The entire manual is important, but this segment may be regarded as its heart and soul. Here, you'll clearly inform franchisees of the everyday procedures for successfully running their franchise. Topics covered should include operating hours, sales (including forms of payment, refunds, product knowledge, customer relations, etc.), emergency/security policies, inventory, pricing, and general outlet administration. Basically, if there are any general, day-to-day operational questions franchisees may have, this section should answer them.

Sales/Advertising

This part of the manual describes both local/regional and corporate advertising strategies, letting franchisees know what their responsibilities are and what their advertising contribution pays for at the corporate and/or national level. This should include clear procedures for planning and placing local advertising. Samples of such things as newspaper and yellow pages display ads may be represented. If appropriate, direct mail and telemarketing procedures should be covered. Promotional contests and themes should be suggested and outlined. Then, too, if direct sales techniques are to be employed, a step-by-step scenario should be described. Finally, this section must spell out what kinds of advertising a franchisee is authorized to use and the procedure for seeking authorization for any advertising *not* provided by you.

Each franchisee should sign a statement of confidentiality for the manual, because the manual contains your complete operations system and trade secrets. It is *lent* to the franchisee during the term of the agreement; it always remains the property of the franchisor. It's a good idea to prohibit *copying* any part of the manual, except as you specifically permit. We also suggest numbering all manuals and keeping a master log of who has what manual. This log can be an invaluable tool if any disputes or discrepancies occur.

As we have said, the manual sets forth the standards for your business that franchisees are expected to meet. With a comprehensive operations manual, an uncooperative or otherwise substandard franchisee can never claim, "But you never told me *that* . . ."

Marketing Your Franchise Program

At this stage in the development of a franchise program, it is time to go to market. In other words, your program will finally be ready to be presented to potential franchisees. The process of marketing a franchise can be broken into three steps: planning, generating leads (inquiries from potential franchisees), and following up on these leads. (All of these steps are building toward the goal of actually *selling and awarding* franchises; that step is covered in the subsection following this one.)

Planning

Before you attempt to sell franchises, you will of course want to know who you should be targeting as potential buyers, how to reach these buyers, and how to best try to appeal to these buyers. This is perhaps the most critical stage in the development of your franchise program; the fact is nothing you do before or after will be quite as important as the selection and support of your first ten (or so) franchisees. If these franchisees succeed, your program will have taken a giant step forward; if they fail because you have chosen them poorly or you are not providing the proper service, you may never be able to get your program back on the right track. As the truism goes, you don't get a second chance to make a good first impression.

What "types" of potential franchisees are there to consider? Here are some broad profiles (you'll find examples of these and others at the start of Chapter 6). "Outplaced" businesspeople often make good candidates for franchisees; they often have the financial means (through savings or severance benefits) it can take to succeed as franchisees. (In fact, during the recession years of 1990–1991, 60 percent of franchisors reported an increase in applications from this type of candidate.) Married couples present another promising pool of potential franchisees; they often have both home equity and "sweat equity" (i.e., the work of running the business themselves) to invest. Two other important groups we have mentioned before are your current store employees and customers; while they are perhaps the most risky category in terms of finances, potential franchisees from this group certainly know and like the business, and often make enthusiastic franchisees.

After you have determined who (broadly) you are going to target as your prime market, the next step is to begin generating leads from these and other candidates.

Generating Leads

The easiest and least expensive, if not the fastest and most targeted, way to begin spreading the word about your franchise program is through indirect methods, such as networking through your professional contacts and advisers (salespeople, suppliers, attorney, accountant, banker, etc.). Send letters to these contacts, letting them know that you are looking for qualified franchisees; ask them to mention your program to friends and associates who might be interested. Another direct method is to post professional-looking notes ("Franchises available—ask for details or call XXX/XXX–XXXX") in your existing outlets.

What these methods do is begin to get the word out that your franchise program exists—it lets people know you're out there and that franchises are available. An even better way of spreading the word is through a dedicated public relations campaign. Mentions of your franchise program in the news of features pages of newspapers and magazines, or coverage on radio and television, can go a long way toward establishing the credibility of your program with prospective franchisees. In the public mind, anyone who can afford it can put an ad in the paper, but only the "deserving" are the subject of news or feature coverage. Of course, the truth of the matter is that while you can't "buy" editorial coverage, a good P.R. staff or person can generate stories through ingenuity, persistence, and originality. It's a very cost-effective method of generating sales leads—and story reprints lend credibility.

While publicity can be a useful tool, it should not be solely relied upon to generate leads. Advertising—usually in newspapers or business magazines—is virtually a requirement to attract a steady stream of potential franchisees. It may be local advertising initially; then, as your program grows, it may develop into both local and national advertising.

On a local level, select a metropolitan (or even a targeted suburban) newspaper whose coverage attracts the type of readership likely to be interested in your franchise program. (Some large-circulation papers even produce an occasional franchising advertising section combining ads and features stories on franchises that purchase ads.) On a regional or national level, try the Thursday *Wall Street Journal*'s Mart Section or magazines such as *Inc., Success,* or *Entrepreneur.*

Holding "seminars" (probably more realistically described as "sales presentations") or open houses, or setting up displays at franchise trade shows (as mentioned in Chapter 4), can also be good ways to attract potential franchisees. Another tool that Don's firm has used successfully for many of its clients is direct mail. This can be very cost-effective if your profile prospect is well targeted.

Prospect Followup

Our recommendation when a call is received is to record the caller's name, address, telephone number, and where/how they heard about the franchise, then a franchise brochure should be immediately sent to the prospect. Haste is of the essence—a sales lead can easily go from hot to cold in less than a week.

Franchise brochures are the main lead follow-up and marketing tools used by franchisors. You'll find a detailed description of franchise brochures (along with valuable advice on how franchises will perceive this brochure) in Chapter 4; now let's look at why the brochure is so important and how to assemble a good one.

A franchise brochure is often your first concrete opportunity to make a real, firsthand, professional impression on your prospective franchisees. An attractive, well-written brochure helps the prospect determine whether to inquire further about your franchise opportunity. It also permits the prospect to share information about your program with spouse, relatives, and professional advisors (such as attorneys, bankers, accountants, etc.). Not only does it have to sell prospects on *your* franchise (as opposed to your competitors), it also must often sell them on the *industry* your business is in. In short, a high-quality franchise brochure is an essential selling tool for a franchisor.

Again, the "how-to" of good franchise brochures can be summed up in two words: Hire professionals. (And, also again, a full-service franchise consultant will likely have a marketing staff that can help you prepare your brochure.) No matter who does your brochure, we offer the following important "dos and don'ts" regarding franchise brochures:

Do	Don't
Get it written and printed professionally	Try to save money at the expense of quality (it will show)
Use upbeat, professional color photography with people in the pictures	Use illustrations (makes the business look "proposed") or photos of deserted-looking, empty units
Give cogent, concise information about the franchise and franchisor	Tell your life story or include other unnecessary information

Use an insert or pullout that can be easily replaced to convey information that can become outdated quickly (such as outlet totals)

Trap yourself into needing completely new brochures each year because of dated information

Prepare the brochure with your specific audience in mind—it should reflect who your target franchises are

Be so specific that you disqualify too many interested people

Use clear, footnoted sources to demonstrate growth and/or trends in your business or industry

Make broad claims about unit sales, projected units, or quick returns

Check the legality of information with a franchise attorney

Let your lawyer write your brochure

Make the tone of your brochure a "call to action," designed to encourage interviews with potential franchisees

Let the brochure become a stodgy "annual report" type of piece without a clear sales message

Make the brochure as complete, honest, and upbeat as possible

Expect the brochure to do all of your sales work

Many franchisors are also successfully using videotaped presentations as part of their lead follow-up process. Done correctly, videos can bring your business to life with motion, music, and special visual effects. They can take prospects behind the scenes with your company and fill them in on details in an entertaining and informative way. If there is "romance" or other visual excitement in your business, you won't find a better way to convey it than through videotape.

And, with interest building and brochures (and perhaps

even videotapes) going out, what comes next? In two words, *selling* and *awarding*.

Selling and Awarding Franchises

All of the previous steps have built up to this one. With decisions made, structures in place, and materials produced, you can finally begin the business of selling franchises. However, the important fact is you are not merely selling—you are also *selecting*. A franchise is not a product, it is a relationship—this is why we say you are both *selling* (convincing the prospect to buy) and *awarding* (granting the franchise to a qualified prospect). This process (when taken to its logical and successful conclusion) roughly breaks down into four stages: (1) The first call, (2) the first meeting, (3) the wait, and (4) the award.

The First Call

Actual selling begins with the first phone call from you or your franchise salesperson to a prospective franchisee, as a follow-up to the materials you have sent. We strongly suggest, at least in the early days of your program, that the salesperson be you; nobody knows as much about your business as you do, nobody will work as cheaply as you will, and the experience will teach you more about your business, about franchising, and about your target franchisees. After all, isn't this the most important task and, therefore, shouldn't it be *your* job?

The purpose of the first call is twofold: (1) To provide information and build enthusiasm about your program, and (2) most importantly, to begin qualifying the prospect.

Qualification—which should continue throughout the sales/awarding process—is important not only as a means of screening prospects in order to select those with a reasonable chance to succeed, but also to emphasize in the mind of a prospect why he or she must meet certain standards and criteria before a franchise will be awarded.

To make the most of that first call, we recommend you begin the qualification process by asking questions designed to provide you with information in three important areas: Financial, readiness, and experience.

Financial

Don't be shy about asking whether the prospect is in a position to afford your franchise: "Mr. X, are you aware the total investment required for this franchise is Y dollars and you will probably need a minimum in cash of Z dollars?" (Most franchisees put down between 20 and 40 percent and borrow the rest.) "Do you have either the borrowing capacity or net worth to be able to handle this kind of investment?" These questions convey immediately that you are both selective and genuinely interested in the success of your franchisees. If it seems the prospect may not initially qualify, you should help the prospect look for alternative ways to finance the purchase: "Do you have equity in your house? Do you have a family member who could go in with you or could cosign a bank note? Would you be willing to consider a smaller market?" If, after exhausting the various possibilities, the prospect simply doesn't qualify on financial grounds, tell her so: "Mrs. X, it doesn't sound like you have the financial capabilities to qualify as a franchisee at this time. However, should that situation change, we'd very much like to talk to you again."

Readiness

A prospective franchisee can be financially well-qualified but still not be fully prepared to move ahead. You should ask the prospect how soon he or she will be ready to seriously begin the process of becoming a franchisee. If the prospect will not be ready within a reasonable period of time (such as six months to a year), it's probably best to delay your meeting with him or her until that point. Too much can change for both parties in that amount of time. Also, you want to devote your full energies and attention toward the prospects that *are* ready to move ahead.

Experience

As demonstrated in the franchisee test in Chapter 3, most franchisors have not found experience in a particular type of business to be an indicator of future franchisee success. So, while you should not necessarily make business experience a hard and fast criterion—instead, balancing your decision by considering the full range of qualifications discussed in that test—you certainly want to know who does or does not have it. The degree of the prospect's experience might not be apparent in a list of his or her previous vocational activities. Specific questions should be asked, such as: "Have you ever held a sales position?" "Have you ever managed people?" and "Have you ever run your own business?"

Those who pass this preliminary screening and who indicate an interest in your program should be invited to a meeting in your offices. Actually, this invitation can be considered a fourth qualifying procedure. A prospect who refuses to come to see you—at the cost of time and perhaps a plane ticket—probably hasn't achieved a level of interest that will enable you to persuade him to commit his money and future to your program. A person who has prequalified in these four areas becomes an excellent prospect indeed; such a person deserves your "best shot" in a face-to-face meeting.

The First Meeting

At the meeting in your offices with the prospect, you will obtain additional qualification information. Persuade the candidate to fill out the full application (if not done already), including extensive business, financial, and reference information, and set up, either that same day or very soon afterward, a schedule of full interviews between the candidate and the other principals in your program. You'll also review all the selling points of your franchise, and probably take the candidate on a tour of a company-owned outlet.

At the first meeting, give the candidate the offering circular (covered fully in Chapter 9), explain its purpose and content, and obtain a signed receipt. (Be sure that receipts are carefully kept, so that no one can claim an offering circular was not provided on the date specified.) Also, stress the fact that no money can change hands for ten business days from the time the candidate receives this document.

This is the time to explain that the franchise agreement is fundamentally a nonnegotiable document, and that franchise laws prescribe that, broadly speaking, all franchisees must be treated equally. And, while it is advisable to have a candidate consult his attorney, it should be clearly explained this involvement is only in an advisory capacity; they cannot regard a franchise agreement as a contract or lease on which they are generally expected to negotiate improvements or compromises.

After the meetings and interviews, you and your executives need to review the acceptability of the candidate, being sure to check the applicant's references and financial status and history. If the candidate is acceptable as a franchisee, notify him or her and set a date for the closing of the sale, keeping in mind the ten-business-day legal limit following the issuance of the offering circular.

The Wait

Buyers often wonder during the waiting period whether or not they are making the proper decision. This is normal. Any big-ticket purchase inspires some amount of buyer's remorse in most people. And, beyond a mere purchase, this transaction represents a huge change in life-style and life for the franchisee-to-be. It is important that you communicate with the buyer more than once during this period to answer any questions and generally provide any reassuring hand holding needed. Your confidence and forthrightness can help convince the buyer he or she is making the correct decision in those days prior to the closing of the sale.

The Award

It is customary for the franchisee and his attorney and the franchisor and his corporate attorney to meet for the closing—the awarding of the franchise to the new franchisee. All that remains is for the agreement to be executed and for the initial franchise fee to be paid. This done, you shake hands. Congratulations, you have a franchisee! You are a franchisor.

And now comes the *real* beginning of your franchise program and the hard work of growing a business.

Making the Program Work

Without disregarding what we have said previously, we believe that selling franchises can be the (relatively) easy part. Making them work is the hard part. And you can't make them work at all unless you have selected the right kind of franchisees and then given them the appropriate training, support, and supervision.

In the period immediately following the sale (and extending through the first few weeks after the opening of the new franchised unit), the franchisor should be accessible to assist the franchisee in site selection, lease negotiations, equipment purchases, selecting initial inventory, and grand opening promotions. (Although these phases apply most cogently for retail franchise outlets, service-oriented franchisees will also require plenty of initial attention and assistance from franchisors.)

The last few days and hours before the franchisee opens her new unit are emotionally (and, often, physically) trying, with the franchisee knowing she has her life savings on the line, wondering whether customers will materialize, and if they do, whether she'll be able to handle them.

But the franchisor should be right there, reassuring and providing last-minute instructions. For the first few weeks or months afterward, a regular schedule of visits should be planned, providing all the assistance the franchisee should need. Additionally, all the franchisee should have to do is pick up the phone and call for answers to specific questions, until the business seems so second-nature that these earlier worries are forgotten. And, as the franchisees become more knowledgeable in the operation of the business, they can no longer be treated as fledglings. The franchisor becomes more of a consultant or a senior partner.

The franchisor should have a planned program of support,

including store visits by the field supervisor, who—initially, at least—may be the founder and/or president, but will be a specialist as the system grows. This supervisor should be available to assist the franchisee, as needed, with supplier relations, employee relations, community relations, and financial matters. The supervisor should also act as a liaison between the franchisee and the franchisor's headquarters to notify the franchisor when the franchisee needs additional support, training, or any other assistance.

Of course, as in any successful relationship, communication is the key. Open lines of two-way communication can help both parties keep abreast of each other's situations. Keeping track of the facts and figures relating to your franchisees is, of course, important, but there are factors to keep in mind that can affect sales figures—location, regional economy, effect of advertising support, and level of competition are just some of the most obvious and critical ones. A franchisor who can understand and appreciate any given franchisee's complete situation is better positioned to maintain a healthy and nurturing relationship with that franchisee.

When Ray Kroc personally visited the first few McDonald's franchises in the early days of the company's franchise program, he often spent a few minutes picking up the trash in the area surrounding the outlet before meeting with the franchisee. He then showed the franchisee the amount of trash that he had found and strongly suggested that the franchisee ought to be paying attention to this kind of detail. His actions not only underscored the importance Kroc put on cleanliness, but it also showed the franchisee and the outlet's employees that the franchisor cared about them and their specific needs. Kroc couldn't help it—he was single-minded about the complete success of each one of his franchisees.

While you need not go as far as Kroc did, if you employ a combination of an understanding of your franchisees' situations, true two-way communication, and firm but reasonable direction, you can help keep your individual franchisees successful.

And, as we've shown, Ray Kroc learned that successful franchisees can lead to successful franchise programs!

Chapter Nine

Franchising and
the Law

Sometimes it seems as if people outside of franchising have one of
two perceptions about the industry's rules and regulations. Either
they believe that (1) franchising is a wide-open, mostly unregu-
lated field where chains seem to spring up overnight and, often,
disappear just as quickly (presumably at the expense of franchisees' savings, dreams, and hard work); or that (2) franchising is a
highly regulated morass of red tape, making establishing or
buying a franchise a long, drawn-out legal hassle.

As it turns out, neither of these extremes is entirely accurate.
The truth lies somewhere in between—yes, franchising is regulated, to protect and inform all parties involved; but the laws are
not so complicated as to place an unnecessary hardship of time or

money on either potential franchisors or franchisees. But, of course, there are important facts to be aware of regarding the laws of franchising.

The topic of franchising legal matters can neither be split completely into franchisor and franchisee components nor seamlessly combined into one simple and all-encompassing manifesto. And, because of the mutual nature of the franchisee-franchisor relationship, it behooves all parties to be aware of the legal rights and restrictions to be found on either side of the relationship.

Accordingly, this chapter is divided into four unequal and, at times, overlapping sections: A general introduction, covering the history and development of franchising laws; legal topics for franchisees; legal topics for franchisors; and answers to commonly asked legal questions about franchising, concerning both franchisees and franchisors.

Flagrant Early Abuses

There is no doubt about it—franchising has grown from its humble beginnings into a broadly accepted, widely successful way of doing business. However, as we noted earlier, before franchising reached its current pinnacle (a lofty peak, indeed, with negligible signs of any coming downturns ahead), it went through a period of "growing pains" during the 1960s and early 1970s. An unfortunate residue of this period was the lingering impression held among some members of both the general public and the business world that franchising and franchised businesses were undesirable and inferior, especially when compared to local businesses in the same field.

A major reason for the fostering of this negative image, which we believe has since been eliminated for all but the most intractable critics, was the appearance during this wild, booming period of a number of unscrupulous franchisors offering dubious or even nonexistent franchises, often cheating investors and consumers alike. A few of these franchising swindles and mismanagements became front-page news of stories about people bilked of their life savings. Some of these questionable businesses also tarnished the names of often unsuspecting backers, most notably entertainment figures such as Minnie Pearl and Jerry Lewis. Pearl, a popular television and country music personality, lent her name to a chain of fast-food chicken restaurants (but, as was typical of these arrangements, she was not substantially involved in the business). The restaurants failed because backers hoped to open a large number of restaurants in a short time but did not establish a strong, standardized operational format for the restaurants once they opened.

Jerry Lewis Movie Theaters were another example of a celebrity endorsement—again, virtually in name only—of a franchise without a comprehensive, well-thought-out business plan. Opened at a time when movie theaters were suffering from the competition of television (especially color television, which was new and quickly growing at the time), the franchise folded.

One franchise failure of this period that received a fairly large amount of media coverage, including an investigative report by the television program *60 Minutes*, was that of Wild Bill's, a hamburger franchise that deceived many hopeful franchisees. The promoters opened one restaurant, then quickly sold franchises for many others. The subsequent franchises were never opened because there was no real support forthcoming from the franchisor. These promoters were excellent salesmen (if not businessmen), as Mike Wallace of *60 Minutes* learned when he interviewed one of the people who lost their savings investing in a Wild Bill's outlet that turned out to be nonexistent. Wallace asked the interviewee, who was a professional with an understanding of business, how he could have been fooled so easily. "If you had been there, you would have bought it too," was the sheepish reply.

In addition to these widely publicized abuses of franchising, the formative years of the industry often saw an emphasis by some franchisors on selling the franchise, not on the product or service to be franchised. Innocently or by design, many franchisors and franchisees encountered problems with misunderstandings, miscalculations, misrepresentations, and even out and out fraud. It was clear that for franchising to survive and prosper, its myriad practitioners (most of whom, to be sure, were running honest systems) needed to be held to agreed-on standards of regulation.

State Laws

In 1971, in response to a growing number of legal irregularities in franchising, California enacted the first state law pertaining specifically to franchise registration. (This is hardly surprising, since, as we have pointed out, California has been a hotbed of franchising and other entrepreneurial concepts, providing a fertile environment for new, innovative, and fast-growing business concepts.) Throughout the 1970s and 1980s, other states followed suit, and, at this writing, the fourteen states listed later in this chapter (plus one Canadian province, Alberta) have adopted rules and regulations requiring that franchisors submit extensive information about the nature of the franchise offering (and the history of the principals involved in making the offer) prior to offering and selling their franchise. This process is commonly called "registration" and the states that require registration are known in the industry as "registration states." In any of these states, franchisors selling franchises are required to register (with some exceptions) if one or more of the following conditions occur:

1. The offer is made from the state
2. The offer is received in the state
3. The offer is accepted in the state
4. The franchisee is domiciled in the state
5. The franchisee resides in the state
6. The franchisee's business will be located in the state

Conceivably, if a Maryland-based franchisor were to meet at an airport in New York a prospective franchisee who is a resident of Illinois and who wanted to discuss buying a franchise that will be located in California, the franchisor would have to be registered in all four states! A little confusing, perhaps, but yet another reason why we continuously counsel the importance of professional guidance for prospective franchisors and franchisees. When dealing with matters of law, this is an *absolute* must. It brings to mind the adage, "A man who acts as his own lawyer has a fool for a client!"

The UFOC and the FTC Rule

The Uniform Franchise Offering Circular (UFOC) was created and adopted in the mid-1970s to meet the needs of the states that required disclosure on the part of franchisors. Essentially, its rules require that franchisors furnish prospective franchisees with very specific information about themselves, the business, and the terms of the franchise relationship.

The FTC Rule came about as a result of years of investigation and work on a number of franchising bills by various Senate committees and by the Federal Trade Commission. Formally titled "Disclosure Requirements and Prohibitions Concerning Franchising and Business Opportunity Ventures," the FTC Rule was finally approved in December 1978, and became effective in October 1979. For the first time, disclosure by franchisors became mandatory in all states, not simply in the registrations states and states with business-opportunity laws. In addition to providing a format for disclosure (although not one as comprehensive as the UFOC), the FTC Rule defines the type of business relationship that is considered a franchise and exempts, among others, such relationships as membership in retail-owned cooperatives and the granting of single-trademark licenses.

The federal government's attempt to regulate franchising activity with the FTC Rule did not diminish the states' authority to do so, and was in fact stated to be a minimum standard on which states could add additional protection as they saw fit. The Rule allows franchisors to comply with the Uniform Franchise Offering Circular in lieu of the FTC format document, provided that either the FTC document or the UFOC guidelines are followed in its entirety.

The penalties for failing to comply with the FTC Rules are

severe, up to $10,000 per violation. In one case, a heating-and-air-conditioning franchisor and one of its officers settled an FTC allegation of franchise disclosure rule violations and misrepresentations by agreeing to pay $3 million in consumer redress and over $1 million in civil penalties. In another case, the FTC obtained a permanent injunction and a judgment for nearly $1 million against an automobile-parts franchisor. The charge: false earnings claims, misrepresentation of available services, and failure to make required disclosures. In addition, states can punish criminal violations, such as fraud, by imprisonment. In 1980, the president of Pie Tree, a Pennsylvania restaurant franchise, was sentenced by an Illinois court to three years in prison for selling a franchise without an offering circular and without registering in the state, as well as for defrauding a franchisee. Most state franchise laws also provide for a private right of action to recover damages.

When selling franchises in states that do not require registration, a franchisor need only prepare an offering circular that meets the requirements of the FTC Rule or the UFOC guidelines. (*There is no federal registration requirement.*) Both documents require extensive disclosure of various facts pertaining to the franchisor's general business history. A franchisor—with the help of an experienced franchise attorney—needs to determine which of these disclosure formats will be less complicated or burdensome, given the nature and history of its business. (More coverage is devoted to this topic in the franchisor section of this chapter.)

Summing Up

While the laws governing franchising, especially those pertaining to franchise offerings, were enacted to regulate and protect the entire industry, it is clear that the disclosure laws are in place mainly to inform and benefit potential franchisees. However, *complying* correctly and thoroughly with these laws is to the benefit of franchisors. Proper compliance will not only help avoid illegalities and penalties, but can also be the important first step in educating franchisees in the background, rules, and regulations of a franchise system.

The standardization and acceptance of these rules, coupled with the pioneering and ongoing efforts of the state laws, have diminished the occurrence of fraudulent franchise offerings. Today, both franchisors and franchisees are better informed about the industry's legal requirements, and consequently, the tarnished image of the 1960s has been supplanted by well-regulated professionalism. This has created an atmosphere of increased trust and confidence that benefits both sides.

Legal Topics for Franchisees

As we have stated, prospective franchisees will want to involve their personal or business attorneys in their dealings with franchisors. But we must make this important point: Prospective franchisees must realize that most things—almost *all* things— contained in an offering circular or a franchise agreement are *not* negotiable. Your attorney will not be able to bargain for a "better" royalty rate or length of term, as you might expect him to try to do with a lease or another business contract, but you *will* want her to look over the documents in question, making certain that everything is as it has been promised, and that no foreseeable surprises appear down the road.

In short, knowledge of the topics covered in this chapter will both alert you as to what you might expect when it comes to the legal end of franchising, as well as provide possibly valuable insights into the franchisor's point of view.

A Look at the Offering Circular

The offering circular is provided to prospective franchisees at the the first personal meeting or ten business days prior to payment of any money or signing of any agreement, whichever comes first. It usually follows the format of the previously discussed UFOC guidelines and basically identifies the major personnel involved in the franchisor's company, provides pertinent business background on these individuals, and explains some important details, requirements, and general provisions of the franchisor's program.

For example, if any of the franchisor's principal officers have declared bankruptcy (or been materially involved with a company which has done so) or have been involved in relevant litigation within a specified time frame, these instances must be noted. Of course, such previous occurrences among a franchisor's leaders does not mean that the franchisor is not worth consideration; the information is required to be disclosed to better assist potential franchisees in making a well-rounded and carefully regarded decision. (However, such "red flags" among a franchisor's offering circular probably mean that you should do some independent research to determine that the franchise *isn't* on shaky financial or legal ground.)

The following are a few other important points to look for in an offering circular. Information about these (and other) items are *required* to be included in this document; if they are not, be sure to inquire why.

Amount of Franchise Fee, Other Fees, and Total Initial Investment

These sections are required to disclose the amounts of the franchise fee, the royalty rate, any additional fees or charges (for such services as site selection or training), and the total amount of the franchisee's initial investment with the franchisor. Often separate from this total figure (because it is not usually paid to the franchisor) is the cost of the outlet's lease or real estate (if applicable) and any required fixtures, equipment, and preopening inventory. If these are *not* included, ask for an estimate of these costs; they could *dramatically* (and unexpectedly) raise the amount of money (and/or credit) you'll need.

Requirements Pursuant to Purchases or Leases

Will you be required to buy equipment and/or supplies from a designated source? Or will specifications for these purchases be outlined, allowing you leeway (in *some* cases) in shopping for these essentials? These requirements must be spelled out. If no suitable explanations are given for certain criteria, ask why; it is not illegal or even unethical to require such purchases, but you are well within your rights to know the reasons behind the decree.

Obligations of the Franchisor

Many promises—both concrete and vague—can be made during a franchise sales presentation: "We'll help you find a good location"; "You'll have the advantage of our buying power to keep your costs down"; "We'll be there to help you market your new outlet." This section of the offering circular lets you know exactly what services the franchisor will provide to you *at no additional cost.*

Commitment of the Franchisee to Participate in the Actual Operation of the Franchise Business

Perhaps you were considering purchasing a franchise as an investment, intending to have a family member on an investor-partner run the business. The information in this section will let you know if this is possible under the franchisor's standard agreements.

Renewal, Termination, and Repurchase

This covers the length of the franchise agreement term, the conditions of renewal and rights of termination of the agreement, and any restrictions concerning resale and/or assignment of the franchise. If you regard your potential franchise as something you can invest in and then sell for a tidy profit or pass on to your children, this section is very important, indeed. Many franchisors limit the conditions under which a franchise can resell or assign a franchise; often, the franchisor retains the right of first refusal when it comes to selling. Be aware that most franchisors use term renewals as a mechanism to enforce current standards or establish new ones as a franchise system grows. This is perfectly within their rights—it's simply good business—and you should realize that the granting of a franchise (at whatever the current standards of operations are) is *not* set in concrete; it can be a fluctuating thing.

Information Regarding the Franchisor's Current Franchisees

This is the most recent list of the names and addresses of the franchisor's franchisees. Contact a sampling of these individuals to ascertain whether they are happy with the franchisor. Were all promises that were made kept? What surprises arose during the first year of operation? There is no more valuable opinion—either good or bad—about a franchisor than the one that can be gleaned from its current franchisees.

Training and Other Assistance

Nearly all franchisors provide some sort of training (if even just minimal setting of guidelines in the case of conversion franchises), but the length of training, the location of the facilities, the likely cost of transportation and lodging, who pays for it (usually the franchisee), and any provisions for problems that may arise (such as failing to complete the program in the prescribed time limit) will vary from franchise to franchise. These points will be explained here, as will information about the level of the ongoing guidance you can expect to receive from the franchisor (if any).

Advertising

This will give you some idea of what your advertising contribution royalty will buy, both in terms of national and local advertising, including materials, packaging, and promotional

materials. Grand opening and basic ongoing advertising requirements are also likely to be spelled out.

Quality and Service Standards

One of the main proven strengths of franchised businesses is their
ability to deliver the same product or service at any location. The
uniform practices and standards that make this possible are
dictated in this portion of the agreement. This includes specifications and requirements for the purchases of supplies and other
material, as well as definite franchise-wide codes of conduct and
policy.

Reasons for Termination

Defaulting on scheduled royalty or fee payments, failure to make
timely submission of reports or financial data, abandonment of
premises (which can even mean closing up for a two-week
vacation!), or just general failure to comply with the terms of a
franchise agreement—these are all typical reasons for the termination of a franchise. Pay close attention to the explanations of
these requirements in the agreement: Most franchisors are not
looking to capriciously pull franchises out from under hard-
working franchisees, but you *do* need to know just exactly what
you have to do to keep your franchise out of the violations that
can lead to termination.

Transferability and/or Sale of Franchise or Death of Franchisee

We've briefly touched on this before, but it is a very important
part of the agreement. In the sections covering these topics, the
franchisor will set the conditions under which it will allow the
franchisee to transfer or sell his or her franchise. As we have
mentioned, if passing the franchised business on to your children
or other family members (whether by choice or due to death) is
important to you, you will want to know if the franchisor will
permit this to occur. Similar requirements will be set for the sale
of the franchise—usually granting the franchisor approval of the

purchaser and often granting the franchisor the right of first refusal, meaning that the franchisor can buy the franchise at the same price as offered by any would-be buyer making a bona fide offer.

Franchisor's Financial Statements

Your franchisor is required to include audited financial statements for its most recent three years of operation, plus unaudited statements of the recent period within ninety days. How healthy is the company? Is the company *just* a franchise company or does the same corporation also own and operate outlets? (Many franchisors start separate corporations to franchise—there is nothing wrong with this but you should know which is which when reading the statements. If company outlets are included you may be able to tell something about the health of the business.)

It is important to remember that the material included in the offering circular has not been checked by any federal agency; in fact, the cover page of the circular states that the material as presented definitely *hasn't* been verified. What regulatory agencies *do* is to provide the framework in which this information must be disclosed. (And, in the case of a later discrepancy and/or legal dispute, they will often check the information for the sake of prosecution or other enforcement.)

Finally, there is a *mandatory* ten-business-day waiting period after the prospective franchisee receives the offering circular, during which *no* money can change hands and no agreements can be signed. Any franchisor asking for your commitment in terms of money or a signed contract or a combination of the two before this "cooling off" period has passed is breaking the law.

The Franchise Agreement

Federal laws and the laws of many states require that every franchise company submit to its prospective franchisees a document that specifies in detail the terms under which franchisor and franchisee will do business together. This contract is commonly known as the franchise agreement. The franchise agreement describes explicitly the entire extent of the franchisor's relationship with its franchisees, outlining the terms and considerations by which the franchisees will be expected to operate their franchises. By establishing standards of operation, the agreement helps to both alert a franchisee as to what is expected of him or her as well as to ensure systemwide uniformity throughout a franchise.

The franchise agreement is given to a prospective franchisee at the same time as the offering circular. An execution copy of the franchise agreement with the material terms filled in *must* be provided at least five business days before it is accepted. Your attorney will want to review the agreement (though as we said earlier, she must bear in mind that she can't negotiate many, if any, of its terms).

A final reminder and warning to prospective franchisees: Before the ten-day period (following the issuance of the offering circular) has passed, even a deposit "just to hold your claim in case any other prospects are interested" or a downpayment "just until we process the paperwork" is *illegal*. No amount of money is to change hands until *the time required by law has elapsed*.

Legal Topics for Franchisors

If you are seriously considering franchising as a means of expanding your business, you should be aware that, as a franchisor, your activities are likely to be regulated far more than they ever have been before. Moreover, the laws that will affect you are *in addition to* those that govern companies not involved in the sale of franchises.

The majority of the most important initial legal matters for franchisors involve properly developing forms that disclose facts about the franchise to prospective franchisees. Paramount among these are the offering circular and the franchise agreement. We have briefly examined these in the franchisees' section, and will cover these a bit more here—but of course it is very important for new franchisors to make use of the assistance of an experienced franchise attorney (preferably working in concert with the legal department of a franchise consulting firm) to outline and generate these documents.

Registration States

We previously mentioned the requirements of registering a franchise program in various states (plus the Canadian province of Alberta). The fourteen so-called registration states are:

California	Michigan	South Dakota
Hawaii	Minnesota	Virginia
Illinois	New York	Washington
Indiana	North Dakota	Wisconsin
Maryland	Rhode Island	

Registration states treat the sale of franchises much as they would the sale of securities. This means (among other things) the franchisor must submit the information to be disclosed in a format approved by the states. This document generally is referred to as the "disclosure document," or more formally as the "offering circular." In some cases, the offering circular and the franchise agreement will be cross-checked at the state level to see that they are consistent with one another and that they are both in compliance with the laws of their states. A few states that do not have franchise laws do have what are known as "business opportunity laws." Some franchise offerings will trigger these laws, but compliance with them will be generally less complicated than in registration states. The laws of the following states are most likely to trigger compliance by franchisors:

Connecticut	Maine	Texas
Florida	North Carolina	
Georgia	South Carolina	

210

In the remaining states, where neither franchise nor business opportunity laws require specific compliances, franchise documents need not be filed with state agencies. Nevertheless, in all states before selling a franchise the franchisor must provide prospective franchisees with an offering circular prepared in accordance with Uniform Franchise Offering Circular guidelines (UFOC) or the Federal Trade Commission Rule, with all relevant agreements and financial statements attached, and according to a prescribed timetable. In addition, of course, the franchisor must meet any other specific requirements imposed by these states.

The UFOC Requirements

Although the UFOC is more comprehensive in its requirements than the FTC, both formats call for disclosure—with differing levels of detail—of a wide range of information. As we stated during the franchisees' coverage of this subject, a properly prepared UFOC includes data on such topics as the identity of the franchisor and any predecessors; the amount of franchisee's initial franchise fee (or other initial payment) and the amounts of any other mandatory fees; trademarks, service marks, trade names, logotypes, and commercial symbols; renewal, termination, repurchase, modification, and assignment of the agreements and related information; and financial statements.

It should be noted that under both the FTC Rule and UFOC guidelines, anyone who has declared bankruptcy or has been a principal officer in a company that has declared bankruptcy must disclose the facts and dates of the circumstances and proceedings if they occurred within a specified period of time. Likewise, a litigation history of listed and "material" actions for the franchisor's principal officers or partners— covering the previous ten years under the UFOC and seven years under the FTC, plus any pending actions (except in California)—must be included. By omitting or materially altering this information, whether intentionally or accidentally, a

211

franchisor could be severely penalized (as we stated, up to $10,000 *per violation*).

The Franchise Agreement

Perhaps no one part of the franchise development process is as important to the ultimate success of the franchise program as the drafting of the franchise agreement. It is essential that an attorney who understands franchising and is familiar with the franchisor's business prepare this agreement, and it's equally important for the franchisor personally to participate in the development of the agreement, because he or she is the most knowledgeable about the circumstances and requirements of the business. This is not the time to save money by copying a "standard" franchise agreement or for "boilerplate" legal work. Each franchise agreement should be as unique as the business it represents. It is the cornerstone of a franchise relationship, and it must be thorough enough to provide both parties with a clear understanding of that relationship.

By all means, you want to avoid the unfortunate situation that many franchisors encounter when a problem arises with their franchisees. They rush to look at their agreements to see if the situation is covered, only to find that it isn't and there is no easy legal remedy. The franchise agreement should also be fair to the franchisee—a well-drafted document will protect the franchisee and will meet with minimal objections from his or her attorney.

The following overview touches briefly on a few of the most important points a well-written franchise agreement should address.

Maintenance and Repair
In the past, franchise agreements frequently lacked any clause requiring the franchisee to maintain his unit to certain minimum standards, as specified in the operations manual. Thus, the manual set forth standards, but the agreement lacked the "teeth"

to enforce these standards. This situation has largely changed, with clauses being inserted requiring franchisees to make certain repairs, upgradings, and modernizations to keep their units up to current standards. In many cases, renewal approval is dependent upon such remedies being applied by franchisees.

Insurance

Many agreements address the provision of insurance minimally or not at all. The franchise agreement should require the franchisee, at the very least, to have general liability, worker's compensation, and property insurance and specify minimum coverages, with the franchisor as coinsured receiving a copy of the policy and any notice of cancellation. "Key man" and business interruption insurance are also often a good idea. The franchisor may wish to recommend an insurance company (frequently the franchisor can negotiate lower rates based on volume), although the franchisee has the right to select his own carrier so long as the policy meets the coverage requirements of the franchisor. Moreover, provisions may require that if franchisees do not obtain proper coverage, franchisors may instead do so, and be immediately reimbursed by the franchisee.

Training

The franchisor's training program is the last stage of the process of qualifying a franchisee. It is important that the agreement state that the franchisee must successfully complete that program, and that if he does not do so the franchisor may terminate the franchise agreement and retain a specified percentage of the franchise fee to offset the costs of initial training.

Advertising

The franchise agreement should require the franchisee to use only advertising materials developed or approved by the franchisor (and state clearly how the materials are to be submitted for approval and to whom). Many franchisors require that franchisees contribute to an advertising fund of joint benefit to all franchisees, which is administered by the franchisor. If this is the case, the agreement should also specify to whom the money should be paid and how often.

Transferability of Interest

In the event that the franchisee wishes to sell his franchise, a clause in the agreement should stipulate provisions under which that can be done, including: (1) Approval of the new buyer by the franchisor; (2) successful completion of training by the new buyer; and (3) payment (in advance) of an agreed-on transfer and training fee to the franchisor. The agreement should indicate that the franchisor will not unreasonably withhold approval of the transfer—but it may also give the franchisor right of first refusal to buy the franchise at whatever price has been offered. Lastly, the agreement should specify, if the franchisee dies, on what terms the survivors can operate the business or sell it, and on what terms the franchisor can acquire it.

Acknowledgement of Receipt of Documents

The FTC Rule states that the prospective franchisee must be presented with an offering circular ten business days before the execution of a franchise agreement or payment of any money, and a completed franchise agreement five business days before acceptance. The franchisor should obtain a receipt for these documents, but receipts are known to have become lost. However, if the *agreement itself* states that the franchisee acknowledges receiving the documents the required number of days in advance (and the parties have in fact waited the requisite number of days), a franchisee who subsequently fails in his business will have extreme difficulty prevailing in a lawsuit against a franchisor on the spurious grounds that the franchisor accepted his money without the proper waiting period or the disclosure of required information.

These and other "small" details of a well-prepared franchise agreement could conceivably save the franchisor embarrassment, expenses, and perhaps even a drawn out, expensive, and image-damaging lawsuit.

In closing this section, we suggest, in all seriousness, that franchisors begin preparing for a lawsuit the day they sign their first franchise agreement. It may sound cynical, but in today's often litigious business climate (with parties on both sides of many situations turning to the courts as a first step, rather than as a last resort of redress), this precaution not only is valid, it is prudent.

Franchisors should document carefully everything they do for their franchisees, keeping comprehensive files and records that indicate every phone call, every question that's answered or dispute that's resolved, every visit to the franchise (even casual ones), and every instance in which the franchisee is not in compliance. Of course, if the franchise is not in compliance, the franchisor should notify him or her immediately, or face the possibility of not being able to enforce compliance later.

As in most business situations, some well–thought out preparation preparing for the worst can end up helping you avoid or at least minimize difficult situations later.

Frequently Asked Questions

Even after studying the FTC Rule, the UFOC guidelines, and assorted state laws, many franchisors and franchisees have specific questions about real-world interpretations and day-to-day implications of this complex web of laws. In our experience, the following are among the most commonly asked legal questions about franchising:

Can Franchisors Require Their Franchisees Purchase Products from Them?

Usually not, but there are exceptions. One key is whether the franchisor's trademark is so closely associated with the product in question that it would be a misrepresentation to offer anything else. For example, Baskin-Robbins is well within its rights to require that its franchisees buy Baskin-Robbins ice cream: Customers, after all, expect it! A less obvious case in point is that of a California franchisor, Soup Exchange, which requires franchisees to buy the franchisor's salad and spice mix. In this example, the franchisor believes that its special recipe is a proprietary formula and trade secret which contributes significantly to the success of its franchise program. On the other hand, a franchisor can require a franchisee to buy products of a certain quality without actually selling those products to the franchisee. Kentucky Fried Chicken, for example, requires that franchisees buy the "secret blend of herbs and spices" for their chicken's coating mix from designated authorized distributors.

Cases in which franchisees have accused franchisors of using their power to force franchisees to buy products from them are known as "tying" cases. The courts have ruled that some tying requirements in franchisor/franchisee relationships violate antitrust laws. However, the courts *have* recognized that the very nature of franchising may lend itself to certain instances where required purchases of products and services will not be an illegal tie. An illegal tie occurs when a franchisor requires that franchisees buy a secondary product in order to be allowed to purchase the primary product of the franchisor. For example, at one time many oil companies would provide gasoline only to service stations that purchased tires, battery, and other automotive accessories from them. After a rash of these "TBA" cases (for "tires, batteries, and accessories") in the 1950s and 1960s, the practice was ruled to be illegal under the Sherman Antitrust Act.

One of the most famous tying rulings was handed down against Chicken Delight by the Ninth Circuit Court of the United States in 1971. At the time, Chicken Delight was not charging its franchisees royalties, but was instead requiring them to purchase equipment and supplies (such as napkins and packaging materials) from the parent company. Franchisees charged that not only were these collateral purchases held to be a requirement of continued operation, but the material was being sold at considerably higher prices than they could have paid for the same items elsewhere. The court agreed with the franchisees' claims, finding this practice to be an illegal tie. The loss of revenue to Chicken Delight contributed to the U.S. company subsequently going out of business.

How Should Franchisors Answer the Prospective Franchisee Who Asks, "How Much Money Can I Make from Your Franchise?"

Stories abound about the franchisor who, in response to such a question, reportedly wrote a dollar amount on a cocktail napkin and showed it to a prospective franchisee, then pocketed the napkin, which was never seen again. (We're willing to bet that the particular dollar amount "promised" thusly was never seen either!) However, a few of those napkin-type notes have turned up in court, and, as we have stated, the penalties for misrepresentation can be severe.

Another misleading practice involves showing a prospective franchisee a graph showing that (for example) at sales of $300,000, the franchisee would earn $50,000; at sales of $500,000, the earning would be $100,000 a year; and with $700,000 in sales, the franchisee could expect earnings of $150,000—when, in fact, the franchisor has *no* units in operation, or perhaps a few, but none with sales even approaching $100,000. The response by legislatures has been to establish specific guidelines for statements about revenues or profitability (described by the term "earnings claims") based upon solid financial criteria.

In 1987, the willingness of the FTC to back up its ruling regarding earnings claims was made abundantly clear to the franchise community. Responding to an FTC complaint that it had misrepresented earnings and profits of its franchisees, Comprehensive Accounting Corporation, a franchisor with more than 350 units, signed a consent decree and, without admitting it broke the law, agreed to pay back franchisees up to $3.5 million in fees. The company had been charged with failing to indicate whether the contracts of franchises being cited as the basis of claimed earnings had similar terms to those being offered; using improper accounting methods in determining average earnings and profits; and failing to disclose that the sample group used in computing average earnings and profits excluded franchisees who had dropped out of the program.

Both the UFOC guidelines and the FTC Rule contain provisions that describe how claims of actual, projected, or forecasted franchisee sales, profits, or earnings can be presented, if the franchisor so desires to make such a claim. The decision as to whether to make an earnings claim at all is a difficult one to make for franchisors. On the one hand, being able to tell a prospective franchise buyer what earnings might reach can be an effective sales tool. However, franchisors are sometimes reluctant to make claims that even imply a promise to the franchisee that achieving the projecting earnings is "guaranteed." The result can be dissatisfaction and unhappiness (and even litigation) if the franchisee's earnings ultimately do not meet what was "promised."

When sufficient historical figures are available, Don's firm often advises franchisors to make carefully considered, conservative earnings claims. (You probably need not go as far as the previously cited example, wherein every outlet in one franchise system was shown to be potentially losing money!) This said, we must note that the majority of franchisors do not make earnings claims, but the growing trend seems to be *toward* making earnings claims.

Accordingly, franchisees should carefully weigh any earnings-based material a franchisor presents. The claims are often either vague and/or meaningless or glowingly positive; somewhere between these poles, the truth is more likely to be found. Also, beware of franchisors who try to avoid the entire subject by telling prospective franchisees that the FTC has made it illegal to disclose earnings—the truth of the matter is simply that it is illegal to make earnings claims in any format *other* than the one prescribed by either the FTC Rule or UFOC guidelines (depending on which format is selected).

Can Franchisors Prevent Their Franchisees from Doing Business Outside of Their Assigned Territories?

That depends upon the type of franchise involved. If the franchisees operate from a fixed location (as is the case with most retail businesses), the franchisor cannot legally prevent them from promoting and selling their goods and services to anyone who seeks to buy them.

However, if a portion or all of these franchises are *not* location-based—if, for example, the franchisees operate sales forces in previously assigned and protected territories—franchisors may greatly limit the franchisees' ability to promote or sell outside of their territories. Or, at the very least, they may provide that owners of adjacent franchised territories be compensated for sales made by other franchisees within their territories according to a predetermined formula.

Can a Franchisor Set the Prices That Franchisees Will Charge Their Customers?

No. The courts have found such price fixing to be anticompetitive. The most a franchisor can do is suggest guidelines for the prices their franchisees will ask for the goods or services they sell. However, franchisors *may* obtain the agreement of franchisees to participate in special regional or nationwide promotions (especially when heavy advertising support is part of the package), wherein products or services are offered at special, standardized prices—for example a 99¢ Big Mac—for a certain period of time.

Can a Franchisor Sell Goods and Services for Different Prices to Different Franchisees?

No, unless factors such as delivery costs (due, for example, to distance) or quantity purchases are involved. In such cases, these factors must be applied equally to all franchises.

Can a Franchisor Compete with Its Franchisees in the Same Territory?

Only if any franchisee in question has not already been granted an exclusive territory in the franchise agreement—*and* if the competition does not cause him economic injury. Under exclusive territorial arrangements, a franchisee has the sole right to open franchises in a particular area—a state, county, city, or whatever region the contract specifies. Most territorial arrangements now cover no more than a radius of a few miles—or, in the case of a big city or an otherwise densely populated area, a few blocks. Taking this thinking to its obvious extreme, since 1969, McDonald's has limited most of its territorial arrangements to the exact street address of the franchise. An exception is if the franchisor specifically reserves the right to compete within that area (e.g., distributing product through other channels of distribution). For instance, many ice cream franchisors reserve the right to sell ice cream in supermarkets in franchisees' territories—but not to sell ice cream cones.

Can a Franchisor Terminate a Franchisee for Not Following a Prescribed Business Format?

Yes, within reason and with qualifications. A franchisor must show good cause for such an action, and, to reduce the threat of litigation, those causes should be clearly spelled out in the franchise agreement and operations manual. (A franchisor cannot expect franchisees to follow their system if they don't know exactly what it is!)

More difficult issues may arise when franchisees assert that certain changes they have instituted reflect their own expertise in responding to the needs of their local market. Such cases may involve slight changes in operating hours to fit a particular area or neighborhood, or even changes in a restaurant's menu to better suit the tastes of a particular region or foreign country. Here, too, the courts—if it comes to that—are likely to look for the degree to which the franchisor's demands are reasonable.

Can a Franchisor Prevent a Franchisee from Taking Down His Sign After a Few Years (to Avoid Paying Royalties) and Operating an Independent Business Using the Franchisor's System?

It depends on the state in which the franchisee is located and the kind of franchise program that is in place. For business-format franchises (*if* the legal documents are poorly drafted), there will typically be "in term" and "post term" restrictive covenants that will prevent franchisees from operating a similar business for a certain period of time within a defined geographic area. The enforceability of such clauses varies from state to state. Conversion franchises are a different and much trickier matter. Franchisees in conversion programs generally already have been established in the particular business before becoming franchisees, and, accordingly, they usually face less restriction and fewer restraints. Again, the particulars vary from state to state, and even from case to case.

When Can a Franchisor Legally Offer Franchises for Sale?

To offer a franchise for sale, a franchisor must first have a properly prepared franchise agreement, offering circular, and financial statements as described above. Depending on the domicile of the company and of the buyer, where the unit will be located, and where the sale will take place, the franchisor may also have to register in appropriate states.

The franchisor must provide every buyer or every prospect with a copy of the offering circular at the first face-to-face meeting at which there is a serious discussion of the sale of this business opportunity or franchise. Even then, as we have said, there is a mandatory wait of a minimum of ten business days before the franchisor can accept any money and before the franchise agreement (and/or other related documents) are executed.

Are There Conditions Under Which a Franchisor Can Sell a Franchise for Different Fees to Different People?

Yes, provided that such variations are disclosed in the offering circular and uniformly offered to similarly situated franchisees. Franchisors can charge a lower franchise fee to individuals who are familiar with their field of business (as opposed to a complete neophyte who requires extensive training). When setting up a franchise program, franchisors may also state an intention to sell a specified number of franchises at an "introductory" price, noting that they intend to increase the price after a specified date or after a certain number of franchises have been sold. (Some states do not allow this.) There are also instances in which a franchisor might sell a multi-unit or subfranchisor program, offering a discount, in effect, for buying more than one unit.

However, the key—as with the previous question about selling goods and services at differing rates—is that all potential buyers must be offered the same opportunity to buy a franchise at that price under those same conditions and that such arrangement must be disclosed in the offering circular. Or, in the recent parlance of international trade and industrial production, the playing fields must be level!

Is "Licensing" the Same Thing as Franchising?

The term *licensing* often is used interchangeably, albeit mistakenly, with *franchising*. All franchises contain at least one license, but not every license is a franchise. In a classic licensing arrangement, the licensor merely gives the licensee the right to use the licenser's name on a product, business, or formula without substantially regulating how the licensee conducts his or her own business. (An example is the granting of rights to allow the Coca-Cola logo or Disney cartoon characters to appear on clothing or other items.) If you decide that for your business to expand successfully your licensee must operate his or her business in a prescribed way, if the licensee pays you more than $500 during the first six months of your relationship, and if you are willing to let him or her use your name, you probably have sold a franchise rather than merely a license. You can call such an arrangement whatever you like, but a rose is a rose is a rose, and, by any other name, you must still confirm to franchise laws!

What Happens When a Franchise is Terminated for Alleged "Noncompliance"?

It depends. From the franchisor's point of view, there must be franchisee contract violation, prenotification of default must be given to the franchisee, and if after a reasonable period of time (the length of time will vary state to state based on the nature of the default) the franchisee fails to cure the default, the franchise is canceled. At that point the franchisee has two options: accept the termination or fight it in the courts or through arbitration. If the franchisee accepts the termination, he or she will arrange to sell the franchise to another party or to the franchisor, or sell the assets of the business to someone. After paying off any liabilities from the asset or stock sale, the franchisee pockets the cash (if any) and moves on to another business. Most franchise agreements prohibit the franchisee from opening a similar business nearby or in the same location for at least twelve months, subject to enforceability on a state-by-state basis. If the franchisee decides to fight the termination, it faces a speedy court order preventing the franchisee from keeping its doors open (thus making it more difficult to sell to others) and is potentially open to a larger claim of damages owed to the franchisor for continuing to use its name, system, and so forth without following its contract or paying for the right to do so.

These are some of the most significant legal issues that confront any franchisor or franchisee. They illustrate, for example, how vitally important it is for franchisors to have thorough and well-crafted legal documents, created by specialists in franchise law; and also how important it is for franchisees to consult with attorneys experienced in franchise laws before committing to a franchise agreement.

On the other hand, legal issues should not dominate the decision-making process of either a franchisor or franchisee. Above all, do not permit legal matters to drive your decision *whether or not* to start or to buy a franchise; these are both business decisions and must be based on the various criteria we discussed earlier—in Chapters 3, 4, and 5 for franchisees, and in Chapters 7 and 8 for franchisors.

The fact is that most franchise laws have been a boon to franchising. They have made franchising a dangerous game for the few people whose principal interest is in making a fast buck and moving on. In our opinion—and, we feel, in the opinions of a vast majority of those in the franchising industry—the cost and time involved in complying with these laws is well worth the improved reputation of franchisors and increased security of franchisees they have instigated.

Chapter Ten

The Nineties and Beyond: The Future of Franchising

The U.S. Department of Commerce has called franchising "the wave of the future." Alan Hald, chairman of MicroAge Computer Stores and a noted futurist, has said, "There is no doubt in my mind that the primary economic battles of the next fifty years will be waged mostly through franchising." In a special report on the future of franchising, John Naisbitt, the author of the popular and influential *Megatrends* books, sees continued growth and increased market shares for franchised chains and individual outlets.

Although the future can never be fully foretold, what *is* most nearly certain is that whatever the future of retailing and business holds, franchising is likely to play an increasingly important part in that future. It has become clear that nearly *any* product or service can be franchised today. From a solid background of previous growth, franchising has reached an impressive position of dominance in the marketplace. But, as they say, the past is merely prologue; the future—as always, an amorphous and unpredictable era—is where the action will take place.

In this chapter, we'll look at some of the things we expect to occur in the coming years. We'll run through some of the facts and figures behind franchising's prolonged "boom" period, we'll look at the growth in foreign expansion (and other important trends likely to present themselves in franchising's future), and we'll examine some of the challenges that still face this increasingly successful form of doing business.

We're not soothsayers, but we can't help agreeing with the predictions about the future of franchising cited in the opening of this chapter. The future of franchising looks promising and exciting—and we're going to show you why.

There's Still Gold in Them Thar Hills

We've mentioned franchising's so-called boom periods. In the 1960s and early 1970s, many of the longtime "superstar" franchises, such as McDonald's, Holiday Inns, Kentucky Fried Chicken, Midas mufflers, H & R Block, and others, experienced their initial spurt of sustained growth. Then, during the 1980s, franchising diversified. Many large chains grew larger and many new chains were founded. It is estimated that approximately *half* of today's existing franchise chains were begun since the late 1970s, with a substantial chunk of these coming since roughly 1983 to 1985. And, by the early 1990s, this second boom was *still* going on, with new franchised chains and individual outlets continuing to open at a healthy pace.

We've pointed out as well that the numbers behind franchising are impressively large—perhaps *surprisingly* large, since franchising is often taken for granted by the very consumers who use it constantly and consistently. Take another look at these facts and figures:

- More than 35 cents of every retail dollar spent in the United States purchases a franchised good or service
- By the year 2000, that amount should rise to more than *half* of every retail dollar
- By 2000 franchising sales will be at or near *$1 trillion* per year
- From 1980 to 1991, franchising's annual sales figures grew from $336 billion to an estimated $758 billion
- For more than twenty straight years, sales from franchised outlets have grown at an average of 10 percent annually
- By 1991, there were more than 542,000 franchise outlets in the United States, a figure that grows from 4 to 6 percent each year
- Franchised outlets employ more than 7 million workers, and are expected to employ *10 million* workers by early next decade
- It is estimated that a new franchised unit opens every 16 minutes of every day

Franchising has become not just an accepted but an *integral* way of doing business across the country and throughout the world. It has also become a familiar part of the American way of life, affecting most of us every single day. Both the distant and recent past have seen glorious times and steady growth for franchising. But what lies ahead?

The figures we've seen and the trends we follow indicate franchising *will* continue to grow. But how? Let's take a look at some of the most impressive and promising trends surrounding the franchising industry.

Franchising Abroad

Although franchising originated in the United States, that has not precluded it from spreading to the far corners of the world. More than four hundred U.S. franchisors (approximately 17 percent of American-based franchisors) have outlets overseas, totaling more than thirty-five thousand franchised units. And, according to surveys, the overwhelming majority of these chains plan to continue opening foreign units. Other figures indicate more than 50 percent of the remaining U.S. franchisors are going to expand to other countries in the near future. Moreover, more and more businesses in other countries are becoming franchisors, and some of them (Body Shop cosmetics, Fast Frame picture framing, Roche-Bobois furniture stores, and Filterfresh coffee service, to name a few), are selling franchises in the United States.

The appeal of franchising seems to be universal. After all, it helps people become their own bosses and it enables businesses to expand. But international franchising is obviously more complex than the home-grown variety. In addition to language barriers, changes in processes, menus, or ways of doing business are required in order to suit local customs or tastes. For example, in Japan, McDonald's calls its mascot clown "Donald," rather than Ronald, to make the name more pronounceable for the Japanese; in Moscow, Pizza Hut offers such pizza toppings as sardines and salmon, to satisfy the Russin taste for salty food.

The franchising of U.S. businesses abroad has been so successful that some U.S. citizens buy franchises outside of the United States (not only in Canada, Mexico, and the Caribbean, but also in Europe and the Far East) in order to obtain the best available locations. However, some foreign branches of franchise chains prefer to have solely native franchisees.

The New Markets for Franchising

Canada, Japan, England, and Australia have traditionally been the leading countries outside of the United States for franchising, but other markets are emerging. Mexico has the potential of being "another Canada" for U.S. franchisors in the very near future. Franchising is also exploding elsewhere in Latin America as the economies of those countries improve due to market reforms. (Don's firm recently opened a licensed branch office in Buenos Aires.) The realization of the unified European Economic Community—many structures of which are already in place, and others will follow throughout the 1990s—is creating an open, barrierless market of more than 320 million people. This will be a prime audience to buy franchised goods and services *and* to buy franchises.

Japan and the entire Pacific Rim are likely to continue growing as franchise markets. In terms of sheer numbers of franchised businesses, Japan will likely pass Canada as the second-leading franchise market (outside of the United States) by early next century, if not sooner. Japan, generally savvy in its own business dealings, prizes franchising for its steady duplication of products, services, and, ultimately, success. Also, much of Japan's population, especially its young consumers, values all things American, making it a perfect target audience for franchised concepts which have been proven in the United States.

Potential Markets for Franchising

It has turned out that free enterprise—led, at times, by franchised firms—was the best weapon ever employed in the Cold War!

During the heyday of the Cold War, many analysts worried about the "domino effect" in Europe, wherein instability or revolution in one nation was feared to affect its neighbors. Today, however, in Eastern Europe and in the former Soviet republics, the term "Domino's effect" might be more appropriate, as franchising spreads from country to country. These new democracies in eastern Europe represent one of the hottest potential markets for franchised goods and services.

In Chapter 2 we covered the story of McDonald's triumphant expansion into Moscow, which attracted huge crowds of curious and excited Muscovites. That famous first was followed near the end of 1990 with the opening of the first Chinese McDonald's, in Shenzhen, near Hong Kong (which has had a McDonald's since 1975). (Kentucky Fried Chicken and Pizza Hut previously led the march into mainland China, with outlets in the Chinese capital of

Beijing.) A crowd numbering approximately ten thousand packed into the Chinese McDonald's on its first day, and nearly ten thousand local youths applied for the unit's 240 jobs. Another victory for the golden arches, capitalism, and, of course, franchising!

It is our opinion that such newly capitalistic areas as eastern Europe, the former Soviet republics, and China *need* franchising to help jump-start their economies by providing proven methods and systems of doing business. Few of their citizens have experience in running businesses in a responsive, nonsubsidized economy. Without the assistance and guidance of franchising, it would likely take years of trial and error for individuals in these countries to achieve substantial success in their own businesses. In effect, then, franchises can be considered the "advance guard" for the necessary switch in these countries to *purely* market-driven economies.

"Reverse Franchising"

As we indicated above, global franchising is already a two-way street. Foreign-based franchisors are expanding into the United States, in effect, selling us back our own ingenuity! Alan Hald, chairman of MicroAge, sees this "reverse franchising" as having a major impact on the future of the industry: "As other nations become adept at franchising a concept or business, rather than just exporting goods, we will see interesting cultural and economical changes. For example, if a Japanese company exports sushi to the United States, money is made for the company and a need is simply served. However, if a sushi restaurant is franchised from Japan to the United States, the product and the knowhow—the particular management techniques—are exported, a flow of money back to Japan (through fees and royalties) is established, and jobs are created and taxes paid in the United States. Franchising can influence changes in social structures throughout the world." A recent example of just this phenomenon is a client of Don's firm, a Japanese noodle restaurant called Goemon. Named after a legendary samurai, Goemon is importing authentic noodles from Japan, but is making plans to have them made in the United States as soon as they have sold enough franchises to produce sufficient demand to justify custom manufacturing.

In conclusion, we see these interconnected trends continuing. In the 1990s—and beyond—franchising will continue its spread throughout the world, as U.S. franchisors proceed to further explore and exploit foreign markets, and as foreign-based franchisors seek to make further inroads to the lucrative (and, as they are likely to discover, *very competitive*) U.S. market. The "one world" that populist politician and author Wendell Willkie predicted in his book of the same name still remains remote, but franchising can take us another step in that direction, as our examination of foreign franchising has shown. Franchising, by fostering the international cross-pollination of business concepts, will make cultural differences less and less distinct. U.S. franchisors are leading the way, but in the next decade we predict that scores of franchisors from many countries will become household names around the world.

Other Trends for the Future of Franchising

Beyond the continuation and growth of foreign expansion (and its mirror-image, "reverse franchising"), we see the following ten trends as emerging in franchising in the coming years:

Increasing Numbers of Companies Will Franchise Their Businesses . . . and More and More Individuals Will Purchase Franchises

Need we expand on these simple statements? The reasoning behind these predictions are those that we have covered extensively throughout this book!

The Aging of the Baby Boomers Will Provide a Healthy Group of Potential Franchisees and Franchisors

During the last decade of this century, the thirty-five-to-fifty-four age group—which, by the year 2000, will *nearly exactly* correspond to the "Boomer" birth years of 1946 to 1964—will grow the fastest among *all* age groups; this group also represents the prime earning years for most adults. Because an estimated *80 percent* of franchise buyers fall into this age range (as we covered in Chapter 7), this group in the coming years—who will have considerable levels of savings and business experience—will likely translate into a large and highly qualified pool of good target franchisees. Additionally, as large numbers of professionals in this age group gain experience and capital, and perhaps start questioning the directions in which their lives are heading, they can also be expected to begin franchising existing and/or new business concepts, meaning this period should also see sustained growth in the number of new *franchisors.*

The Most Successful Franchises Will Adapt by Modernizing, Introducing New Concepts, and/or Otherwise Changing

As Bob Dylan once sang, "The times they are a-changin'." And as times change, the franchises with the best shot at success are the ones that can roll with the changes. For example, PIP Printing has virtually reinvented itself in recent years. As high-speed, high-quality copying became commonplace in even the smallest of offices (reducing the demand for quick printing), this franchised chain shifted a large part of its business into small-run business printing (such as business cards, forms, and promotional pieces). This took a lot of faith and some further capitalization for their franchisees, but it has allowed the chain to evolve rather than to stagnate and, perhaps, fade away.

Another case for change is the continued "graying" of America. As the elder population of this country grows, franchisors should look for new ways to meet their needs, which may mean changes in the way existing businesses operate, as well as the possible creation of entirely new franchises. (Service-oriented franchises will be in the forefront of those serving the growing elderly population—more coverage on this below.)

To bring up one final McDonald's example: McDonald's is a good illustration of a successful chain that is not content to rest on its laurels, however considerable they may be! Among the products or concepts McDonald's has recently tried or implemented are the long-developed, much-ballyhooed low-fat McLean Deluxe burger, which has garnered a flurry of press coverage; a heavily promoted McJordan burger, endorsed by basketball superstar Michael Jordan; a praised recycling and trash-reduction program; low-fat shakes and frozen yogurt desserts; and a "value menu" offering permanently reduced prices on hamburgers, cheeseburger, combination meals, and other items. In single-incidence examples that may (or may not) point to future changes in the chain, McDonald's has also allowed a unit in Troy, New York, to convert to a self-service, cafeteria-style outlet, and opened a small-town, 1950s-style diner called the Golden Arches Cafe in Hartsville, Tennessee. All of these are in addition to the test-marketing of pizzas, salad bars, and various other products and services that are ongoing at selected McDonald's outlets. You might think if any chain could "coast" on its accomplishments, it would be McDonald's, but instead the king of the hill is working hard at maintaining and even improving on its preeminence.

Service-Oriented Franchises Will Be the Segment of Franchising with Perhaps the Greatest Chance to Achieve Success in the Coming Years

While hamburger stands and frozen yogurt shops are by no means going to wither away in the coming years, we feel the greatest growth in the near future of franchising will be found among businesses offering a variety of *services*. Chief among these are likely to be those franchises providing services for elderly people and two-paycheck families (such as health care, house-

keeping, delivery-making or errand-running, and other custom-
ized personal services), and for businesses (such as printing/
copying, temporary personnel, accounting/tax preparation, and
other information- or technology-based services). These services
will be positioned as being able to free up leisure time or work
time that would be better spent on more specialized projects.

The Naisbitt report mentioned above predicts that service
businesses will grow at an even faster rate than fast-food
restaurants (and other "traditional" franchises) during the next
decade. A study conducted by Don's company, Francorp, showed
that nearly 50 percent of the fastest-growing franchise chains in
the country were involved in service-related fields. Additionally,
many of these service-related franchises are the type which can be
run out of a franchisee's home, making them an attractive
low-cost, high-convenience investment.

Corporate Restructuring and the Quest for New Profit Centers Will Result in Acquisitions of Company-Owned Chains and the Subsequent Resale of the Individual Units of These Chains to Franchisees.

This is similar in concept to the 1980s practice of the "leveraged
buyout": buying a company and selling off its assets and/or
divisions to pay the acquisition cost. The "franchised buyout"
approach has two important differences: (1) The perception of
these transactions are likely to be of "rescue" rather than of
"greedy, mercenary salvage" (as the 1980s dismantlings were
often judged); and (2) the selling-off of these units will not reduce
the size of the company or dilute its strengths and/or market
share. Once the chain is acquired, the individual outlets may even
be sold to franchisees at a higher total price than the original
buy-out, generating instant profit, establishing ongoing income
(from royalty payments), and resulting in hands-on, attentive unit
management from the new franchisees. Thus, profits are made,
stability is established (or restored) at the unit level, and a new,
strong franchise chain is created.

Franchisors and Franchisees Will Expand into Each Other's (and Outside) Businesses

Franchisors will diversify by owning franchises (in other words, by becoming franchisees themselves), by buying other franchisors, or by developing new franchises. Franchisees (particularly franchisees of *large* territories or subfranchises) will diversify by becoming franchisors of new concepts or by becoming franchisees of more than one business (in cases where this is allowed by the franchise agreement or the original franchisor).

More Institutional Money Will Be Attracted to Franchising Companies

After the shake-outs of the 1960s and the continued impressive growth of the last decade, a growing number of institutional investors, such as potential stockholders or investment corporations, are in general pumping large amounts of money into various franchise ventures. We believe, as franchising continues to grow and gain further acceptance in financial fields, that even larger numbers of banks and venture capital firms will commit funds to franchisors, franchisees, and various combinations thereof (such as subfranchisors or franchisees developing large territories).

Conversion Franchising Will Grow in Dramatic Proportions

Conversion continues to be the answer in fragmented industries that lack an identity—and, more importantly, a clear market leader—and need a unified approach to give the concept an edge in the marketplace. In addition, more and more franchisors will offer low-cost conversion options to existing businesses simply for the purpose of growing more quickly (and helping those businesses survive today's competitive marketplace). Research done by Don's firm indicates that in the past couple of years the number of franchisors offering conversion programs has increased by as much as 300 percent.

More Franchisors Will Be Acquired by Large Companies

By acquiring proven franchisors, corporations will seek to reap the benefits of franchising while avoiding many of the pitfalls of entering an unfamiliar market cold. However, this method is not foolproof—costly mistakes can occur due to lack of proper vision, ignorance of a new field, or the replacement of entrepreneurial spirit with corporate bureaucracy.

Also, some corporations have seen franchises as logical outgrowths of their current business. For example, PepsiCo owns Pizza Hut, KFC, and Taco Bell—and not only do these chains turn a profit on their own for Pepsi, but they also provide dedicated outlets for such parent-company products as Pepsi, Diet Pepsi, Mountain Dew, and Slice soft drinks.

Franchising Will Streamline Business the World Over and Give It a More "Human Face"

Management theorists from Peter Drucker to Tom Peters have been preaching for years that corporations need to "get closer to the customer," "flatten out the organization structure," and "learn to manage rapid change." Franchise companies accomplish all these goals automatically:

- You just can't get any closer to your customers than by having an owner at or near each location.
- Franchisors' organization structures are intrinsically flat because they don't need the layers of management that traditional organizations require (see Chapter 7).
- And the vested interest of each franchisee in *getting* and *keeping* customers makes franchise companies quick to respond to changes in market conditions. Remember the research that showed franchisees manage better than company employees? Remember the Big Mac?

By harnessing the entrepreneurial energies of a wider and wider pool of people who want to be their own boss, franchising could well be the new and preferred way of organizing all kinds of companies in the decades to come. What the invention of the assembly line was to business and society in the twentieth century, franchising could be for the twenty-first. And unlike the dehumanizing effect of the assembly line, franchising with its empowerment of local management will *humanize*.

Once again, American business has something it can teach the Japanese—and the rest of the world!

Future Challenges

For all of the rosy predictions of continuing success and all of the promising trends concerning franchising, it *does* face a number of serious challenges. While none of these challenges appears to be a threat to the basic soundness of franchising as an industry, each must be dealt with by both franchisors *and* franchisees for franchising to reach its highest possible potential in the years to come.

As we see them, four of the most important challenges that franchising must deal with (now and in the immediate future) are maintaining franchisee and franchisor standards; maintaining franchisee/franchisor relations; dealing with a changing group of franchisees; and dealing with a changing work force.

Maintaining Franchisee and Franchisor Standards

Ironically, one of franchising's chief advantages also has the potential to be one of its biggest problems. The fact that it is relatively easy to start a franchise—and even easier to *buy* one—will, unfortunately, always attract at least *some* undercapitalized and unprepared franchisors and franchisees; there still will be examples of unscrupulous franchisors and unsophisticated franchisees, despite years of regulatory efforts and the enacting of hundreds of laws to help avoid such occurrences. To minimize the effects these "undesirable parties" can have, we again return to a word we have used many times throughout this book: *research*. By thoroughly checking out the background of a prospective franchisee or franchisor, you can be more sure that you are making the right choice. While there can never be a guarantee that any given franchisee or franchisor will not fail, sufficient research can help protect the prudent franchisee or franchisor.

Maintaining Franchisee/Franchisor Relations

The differing levels of relationships between franchisors and their franchisees can be as large as the number of franchise systems in existence. (And, of course, some of these relationships are in better shape than others!) We believe in the Ray Kroc maxim that to be a successful franchisor, you must have successful franchisees. And, all other things being equal, the franchisee with the best chance for success is the franchisee who is satisfied with the relationship with his franchisor. How is this satisfaction best achieved? Usually by maintaining open and responsive lines of communication, and by allowing franchisees to make active, substantive contributions to the running of the franchise system.

Of course, there is a tendency among franchisors, anxious to maintain strict control over their systems, to be reluctant to share decision-making responsibilities with their franchisees. But history has shown that franchisors who do not allow some level of genuine participation and input from their franchisees may be in for a bloodbath, as franchisees revolt, hold out payments, or even sue—particularly in cases where franchise agreements are not renewed, royalties are raised, or marketing and/or advertising strategies fail (or do not produce the level of desired and *expected* results). To avert these sorts of problems, we believe that savvy franchisors should treat their franchisees as partners and continue to support franchisee groups or associations (whether loosely defined or professionally organized) and involve them in long-term corporate planning. Those who do not may face ruinous court battles in terms of time, money, and reputation as franchisees attempt to flex their collective muscles.

Franchisors also need to work harder to offer their franchisees support and service that is truly valuable. Executives from Don's firm, Francorp, recently attended a meeting for franchisees of USA Baby (also known in some locations as The Baby's Room), a retailer of juvenile furniture and accessories. In a single day of the three-day gathering, the following were among the presentations offered:

- An introduction of new products whose points of value and difference were explained in detail and whose prices were significantly lower than would be likely found at most of the chain's competitors (due to USA Baby's mass buying power)
- Tips from a professional design consultant on working with parents (and even older children) to help them realize their decorating desires with materials from USA Baby stores—adding value to the chain's merchandise
- Plans for adding products and services for a wider age range of children—helping to expand the chain's target customer base beyond the parents of infants
- Exploration of an in-bound telemarketing program to pass customer leads directly to individual stores at a price per lead much lower than could be achieved through separate local programs

These programs and others help USA Baby/The Baby's Room franchisees do their jobs more efficiently and, potentially, more profitably. Such tending to details by franchisors can keep franchisees informed, productive, and happy—which, of course, only helps the bottom line (financially and corporately) of the franchisor. More synergy!

Dealing with a Changing Group of Franchisees

Not only are a large number of baby boomers entering their prime income-earning years, but new opportunities are presenting themselves to groups who had been previously underrepresented in the business world. Women and minorities are increasingly turning to franchising as a way to enter or advance in the business world—and smart franchisors have been only too happy to accommodate them.

Such franchisors as KFC, Burger King, Pizza Hut, Taco Bell, and Baskin-Robbins all have minority recruitment programs for franchisees, offering special financing options and other incentives. It's good public relations and reflects a level of social responsibility, but it's also good business, since these minority franchisees can often help capitalize on inner-city markets. Other franchise programs have been very successful in recruiting women. The Diet Center claims that 98 percent of its franchisees or subfranchisees are women. Women At Large, an exercise franchise aimed at overweight women (who often feel uncomfortable at, or are otherwise not well served by traditional health clubs), has also sold nearly all of its franchises to women.

As the general level of employment among women and minorities rises, and as women and minorities climb through the ranks of the corporate world, more and more of them will gain the experience and the capital needed to enter franchising in even larger numbers.

Dealing with a Changing Work Force

Another irony of franchising is that while it will likely be successful in creating more jobs (up to *2 million* new jobs in the next ten to fifteen years, by some estimates), there may not be anyone who wants to *fill* these jobs.

The American economy continues to change rapidly from being product oriented to service oriented. The Naisbitt franchising study predicts that, before the end of the century, three-quarters or more of the U.S. work force will be in service-industry jobs. Many of these jobs will, quite frankly, be low-paying and offer little in the way of advancement—the kinds of jobs traditionally done by teenagers just entering the work force. But, with the youngest members of the baby boomer generation already entering their thirties—and the expected baby boomlet (children of boomers) somewhat slow in coming—there are fewer and fewer teenagers to take these jobs. In many areas of the country, fast-food restaurants (and other businesses who have a history of utilizing this pool of workers) are already having difficulty in filing these sorts of positions—even (in many cases) when offering salaries well above the minimum wage.

To offset this change, franchisors and franchisees will have to look to other segments of the population to find their employees, including housewives (who may have little or no work experience outside of the home), handicapped individuals, and senior citizens. Franchises may also have to begin offering incentives other than pay—including, for example, scholarships for teenage workers, day-care facilities for working mothers, and improved health benefits and more frequent rest breaks for older workers.

The trend toward specialization in retailing will add another complication to this changing work force because sales clerks will be required to be much more knowledgeable about their products (and, in some cases, much more knowledgeable about computers and other high-tech equipment). Franchisors will be faced with the task of designing programs that are easily understandable and easily replicable, and establishing operating methods that are acceptable not only to the franchisee and to the consumer, but also to the industry's work force.

Franchising itself may also be part of the answer to this problem. How? Look at Coverall, a franchisor of janitorial services, which has grown to over two thousand franchises in seven years, and has expanded expansion into Europe. Part of their secret is a franchise program where subfranchisors develop a territory (selling cleaning services to building managers and large employers), then sell off individual "jobs" (cleaning customers) to individual franchisees who do the work for a fee. In other words, Coverall has converted jobs that people don't want to do for wages into franchises that an *owner* is glad to do because he or she is earning wages *plus* a return *plus* building equity.

Into the Future

Some say, in praise, that franchising has made the world a "smaller place" by bringing peoples and places closer together, linking them with the binding force of successful commerce. Strictly speaking, this may be true, but we prefer to think of franchising as *enlarging* the world—as broadening the horizons and the dreams of people here and abroad.

Franchising has exported distinctly American ways of doing business throughout the world, bringing with it prosperity, prestige, and employment. We also believe, as MicroAge's Alan Hald does, that franchising will also allow other countries to export *their* ways of doing business into the United States and other countries around the world.

Franchising has given countless people the opportunity to realize their dream—whether that dream is to successfully clone a business in various locales or is to simply (but not *merely*) own a thriving business. We think the message is clear: If you're interested in franchising your business or in acquiring a franchised outlet, it's not too late. The wave of the future continues to roll on unabated.

We believe the time is ripe and that the boom still has far to go. We've given you some history, some information, and some predictions. The rest is up to you.

The future looks good for both potential franchisors and franchisees. The future is there for the taking, and the time to act is now. Remember: The future can begin as soon as today!

Appendix I

Categories of Franchises

Accounting/Tax Services
Accounting
Bookkeeping
Electronic tax filing
Income tax preparation

Advertising/Direct Mail
Direct mail advertising
Indoor adboards

Auto and Truck Rentals
Cars
Trailers
Trucks
Vans

Automotive Products and Services
Accessories
Air conditioning
Alarms

Alignment
Auto glass replacement
Batteries
Brakes
Car washes
Dent repair
Detailing
Engine installation
Lubrication
Mobile auto inspection
Mufflers
Oil change
Paint
Paint protection
Parts
Radiators
Rustproofing
Stereo installation
Stereo sales
Sun screens
Tires
Transmission
Tuneups
Upholstery
Used auto sales
Windshield repair
Wiper installation

Bookstores

After-school learning centers
Children's books
New books
Religious books
Used books

Business Aids and Services

Business brokers
Business consulting

Business forms
Check acceptance service
Coffee service
Computerized office systems
Fax
Financial management
Management training and
    development
Mystery shopping service
Office centers
Office supplies
Payroll
Stationery
Telephone answering service
Word processing

Campgrounds

Check Cashing/Financial Service Centers

Check cashing service
Money orders
Wire transfers

Chemicals and Related Products

Children's Services

Clothing
Computer classes for children
Dance programs
Early childhood education
Education
Furniture
Music
Nanny referral service

Clothing and Shoes

Clothing
Footwear

Lingerie
Shoe repair
Socks/Hosiery
Sportswear
Tailoring
Computer/Electronics
Computer rental
Computers
High-tech equipment
Laser printer service
Construction/Remodeling Materials and Services
Bathrooms
Closets
Chimneys
Decks
Gutters
Kitchens
Remodeling
Repairs
Restoration
Water-control systems
Waterproofing
Convenience Stores
Cosmetics
Makeup
Nail care
Perfume and cologne
Skin care
Dating Services
Dental Centers
Drug Stores
Educational Products & Services
Career schools
English education

Human resources
Modeling
Safety education
Time management
Employment Services
Permanent
Professional
Specialized by field
Temporary
Fire Protection Products and Services
Florist Shops
Food
Bagels
Bakeries
Barbecue
Beverages
Breakfast
Cafes
Candy
Cheese
Chicken
Chinese
Cinnamon rolls
Coffee
Cookies
Croissants
Delis
Doughnuts
Family restaurants
French fries
Groceries
Hamburgers
Health food
Hot dogs

Ice cream
Japanese
Meat
Mexican
Muffins
Pasta
Pizza
Popcorn
Roast beef
Sandwiches
Seafood
Snack food
Steak
Submarine sandwiches
Turkey
Yogurt

Home Inspection

Prepurchase inspection
Radon detection

Hotels and Motels

Insurance

Janitorial Services

Commercial
Residential

Laundry and Dry Cleaning

Lawn, Garden, and Agricultural Supplies and Services

Maid and Personal Services

Maintenance, Cleaning, and Sanitation

Cleaning
Drain cleaning
Fire and flood restoration

Leak detection
Window washing

Optical Aids and Services

Package Services

Courier service
Freight forwarding
Packaging
Postal service
Shipping

Pet Sales, Supplies, and Services

Accessories
Dogwashing
Pet sales

Photography

Photofinishing
Portrait studios

Printing/Photocopying Services

Binding
Business cards
Desktop publishing
Photocopies
Typesetting

Formal Wear Rental

Hair Salons and Services

Barbers
Family hair care
Hair replacement
Value-priced hair care

Health Aids and Services

Aerobics
Diet control

Categories of Franchises

Electrolysis
Health spas
Hearing aids
Home health care
Nursing service
Weight loss

Home Appliance: Sales, Rental, and Repair

Home Furnishings

Accessories
Beds
Cabinets
Carpeting
Framing
Furniture
Interior decorating
Paint
Wallpaper
Window coverings

Publications

Real Estate Services

Recreation and Entertainment

Boat rentals
Golf retail
Tanning equipment
Tennis equipment

Retail Stores—Miscellaneous

Art supplies
Balloons
Bath shops

Boxes
Cameras
Clocks
Cooking supplies
Crafts
Cutlery
Gift stores
Greeting cards
Imports
Jewelry
Music
Party supplies
Pawnshops
Sports novelties
Swimming pools
T-shirts
Television
Tobacco
Water

Security Systems

Sign Products and Services

Telecommunication Services

Telecommunications
    equipment
Voice messaging

Tools and Hardware

Transportation Services

Travel Agencies

Video/Audio Rentals and Sales

The Franchise Agreement Topic Outline

A federal law and the laws of many states require that every franchise company submit to its prospective franchisees a document that specifies in detail the terms under which franchisor and franchisee will do business together. Perhaps no one part of the franchise development process is as important to the ultimate success of the franchise as the drafting of this document, commonly known as the franchise agreement.

A good franchise agreement not only incorporates all of the elements of a sound business contract, it expresses in legal terms business decisions vital to the proper operation of the franchise. The following checklist of topics is derived from the examination by Francorp attorneys of hundreds of franchise agreements and the drafting of hundreds of others. It can be used both as a guide to business decisions needed by every new franchise company and as a format for the agreement itself.

1. Appointment and franchise fee

2. Location
  a. Right to approve sites
  b. Right to prime lease
  c. The lease to franchise agreement
  d. Plans and specifications
  e. Equipment must conform to specifications

3. Proprietary marks
  a. Use of name
  b. Contest of name
  c. Notification to franchisor of other's use of name
  d. Conformance to operations manual
  e. Use products, systems, supplies as specified
  f. Sign requirements

4. Training and assistance
  a. Must complete training
  b. Start-up assistance

5. Franchisor's ongoing operations assistance
  a. Continuing advisory service
  b. Promotional materials and bulletins, marketing developments, products and techniques

6. Advertising
  a. Approval of all advertising copy, materials, packaging, promotional materials
  b. Establishment of national advertising fund
  c. Local advertising
  d. Co-op advertising
  e. Grand opening advertising requirements

7. Operating manual
   a. Must adhere
   b. Confidential
   c. Property of franchisor

8. Confidential information
   a. Knowhow, techniques, product formulas are trade secrets
   b. Protection necessary

9. Maintenance and repairs
   a. Maintenance and repairs
   b. Create fund for refurbishing

10. Accounting and records
   a. Must keep complete records as prescribed
   b. Provide for reports
   c. Allow for inspection of records
   d. Provide for auditing statements
   e. Periodic reports and payments of royalty

11. Standards of quality and performance
   a. Establish need for uniformity
   b. Provide for purchases which conform to specifications
   c. Dictate type, quality, and quantity of purchases

12. Modification of system
   a. Establish right of franchisor to modify
   b. Prohibit franchisee from unauthorized modification

13. Continuing services and royalty fee
   a. Establish royalty
      1) Determine program necessary to provide ongoing support and consulting service
      2) Project total direct and indirect costs of providing continuing services
      3) Establish percentage of royalty and continuing services fee to provide for costs and reasonable

return for use of franchisor's name, concept, and system
    4) Ensure payment of royalties

14. Insurance
  a. Protection for franchisee and franchisor
  b. Establish amounts of protection necessary
    1) Workman's compensation
    2) General liability, products, bodily injury
    3) Property damage
    4) Other

15. Determine term
  a. Renewal and termination provisions must comply with laws
  b. Renewal conditioned on updating image of facility
  c. Coordinate with lease
  d. Long term
    1) Ensures royalty longer to franchisor
    2) More security for franchisee
  e. Short term
    1) Adjust royalty upward if desired
    2) Eliminate undesirable franchisees
    3) Allows for earlier execution of new terms and conditions

16. Covenants
  a. Establish restrictions on franchisee's ability to compete, divert business, hire away employees, divulge secrets—subject to state and antitrust laws
  b. Franchisor's remedies

17. Termination and defaults
  a. Bankruptcy
  b. Notice to cure—varies from state to state
  c. Failure to pay royalties or fees
  d. Failure to submit reports or financial data
  e. Vacation or abandonment of premises

    f. Failure to comply with franchise agreement
    g. Injury to system and marks
    h. Loss of license

18. Right and duties of parties upon expiration or termination
    a. Franchisee must pay all sums owing
    b. Franchisee must cease using name
    c. Franchisor's right to purchase physical assets
    d. Franchisor's right to signage and items identified by marks

19. Commencement and hours of operation
    a. Specify when agreement commences
    b. Determine hours and days of operation short of agency relationship

20. Transferability of interest: Provide conditions under which franchisee can sell
    a. Transfer fee
    b. Right of approval
    c. Payment of fees and sums
    d. Approval not unreasonably withheld
    e. Require training of new franchisee

21. Death of franchisee
    a. Survivors can apply to continue
    b. Survivors can sell
    c. Franchisor can buy assets and real estate
    d. Provide formula for buy-out

22. Right of first refusal
    a. Franchisee must notify franchisor of bona fide offer
    b. Franchisor can buy at same price as buyer

23. Operation in event of disability or death
    a. Franchisor's right to operate
    b. Save harmless

24. Taxes and permits
  a. Require payment of taxes, assessments, liens, and equipment, previous accounts
  b. Require compliance with all federal, state, and local laws
  c. Require obtaining of all permits, certificates, and licenses necessary

25. Independent contractor
  a. Not agent, partner, employee of franchisor
  b. Can't incur liability to franchisor
  c. Franchisee bears cost of defense of claims

26. Nonwaiver
  a. Nonenforcement by franchisor is not a waiver
  b. Receipt of payments not a waiver

27. Notice
  a. Manner of notice
  b. Date of notice

28. Liability for breach enforcement: Payment of costs, attorneys' fees by party in default

29. Entire agreement
  a. Overrides any previous agreements
  b. Provides for amendments, changes, or variance only if in writing

30. Severability
  a. Each section of agreement is severable
  b. Franchisor can terminate agreement if parts found illegal affect basic consideration of agreement

31. Applicable law
  a. Specifies which state's laws apply

32. Arbitration (where and when applicable)
  a. Provides for selection of arbiters
  b. Binding arbitration

33. Franchisee acknowledges receipt of FTC or UFOC documents

34. Define term "franchisee" to include successors and all parties of interest

35. Caveat
    a. Disclaimer as to claims made
    b. Franchisee assumes risks
    c. Success of business cannot be guaranteed
    d. Success of business also depends on franchisee's ability
    e. Disclaimer re: FTC Rule and disclosure

Franchise
Operations Manual:
Preliminary Outline

i. Title/Copyright Page

ii. The Franchise Operations Manual
   A description of how the manual should be used and how
   it will be updated

   Statement of Confidentiality
   A one-page statement of the franchisee's responsibility to
   keep the manual confidential; to be signed and returned
   by the franchisee

   Notice of Policy/Procedure Change
   The form used to notify the franchisee of a change in a
   policy or procedure

Submitting Suggestions to the Franchisor
   Instructions for using a form to submit suggestions to the franchisor

Limitations of This Manual
   A disclaimer notifying the franchisee of the responsibility to know and comply with local laws and regulations applying to his or her business

A. INTRODUCTION

Letter from the President
   A one-page letter that welcomes the franchisee to the network

History and Philosophy of the Franchisor
   A one- to two-page discussion detailing when and why the business was founded, who founded it, how the public has accepted it, and where it is going.

Services of the Franchisor Organization
   A brief description of the services provided by the franchisor (training, advertising, operational consulting, enhanced purchasing power, etc.) taken from Section XV of the Franchise Agreement

Responsibilities of a Franchisee
   A list of the responsibilities a franchisee must meet

Visits from the Corporate Office
   An explanation of how the franchisor will periodically monitor franchisee compliance with the system and assist the franchisee with operational issues; includes a description of the role of the person who will be conducting the visits from the corporate office and the phone number

Field Visit Confirmation Form
   A sample form that will confirm that an area representative has conducted a visit with a franchisee

Franchise Survey Form
> An objective and/or subjective form used to assess franchisee compliance with the standards of the franchisor

B. ESTABLISHING A BUSINESS

Introduction

Your Status As an Independent Contractor

Recommended Bank Accounts
> A discussion of the types of accounts each franchisee should open (e.g., payroll, checking, savings, etc.)

Selecting and Developing Your Site
> An outline of the specific criteria franchisees should apply when selecting a site, and the procedure to follow to secure approval of the site from the franchisor

Required Lease Inclusions
> A list of the specific lease provisions that must be included in the lease before signing; based on franchise agreement provisions

Required Insurance Coverages
> A list of the insurance coverages the franchisee is required to obtain

Decor Specifications
> A listing of the decor standards that must be complied with in order to standardize the business's look and image

Signage Specifications
> The specifications that must be met to standardize signage

Required Equipment, Fixtures, and Supplies
> Lists of the required equipment, fixtures, and supplies (and their specifications) that are needed to operate a store

Recommended Initial Inventory
  A listing of the recommended initial inventory needed to open a store

Conducting Your Grand Opening
  A reiteration of the required amount of money expended on grand opening activities, as required in the franchise agreement, and a discussion on how the franchisee should go about planning and conducting grand opening events

Paying Taxes
  A discussion of the federal, state, and city taxes each franchisee will need to pay

Paying Additional Fees
  A description of other fees that a franchisee may incur during the franchise relationship; taken from the offering circular

C. PERSONNEL

Introduction

The Policy on Fair Employment Practices
  A full discussion on the EEOC guidelines

  Inappropriate Preemployment Inquiries
  A list of the types of questions that should be avoided when interviewing applicants

Wage and Labor Laws
  The federal laws governing wages and hours

Sexual Harassment
  Definition of sexual harassment and franchisor's policy regarding it

Complying with the Immigration Reform and Control Act of 1986
  How to comply with the Act; includes sample of the I-9 form

Profile of a Franchisee Employee
A listing of the characteristics and background of an ideal employee

The Recruitment and Selection Process
A full discussion of recommended employee recruitment techniques (e.g., classified ads, present employee referrals, etc.) and the subsequent interviewing techniques for screening applicants

Sample Classified Ad for Recruiting Personnel

Sample Application for Employment

Protecting the System
Discussion addressing the advisability of having employees sign a nondisclosure and noncompetition agreement

The Nondisclosure and Noncompetition Agreement
A sample agreement

The Trial Period
A description of the length of the new employee's probationary period and how this period should be handled

Job Descriptions
Job descriptions for each staff position

Orientation and Training of Employees
General guidelines for getting employees off to best possible start

Scheduling Employee Work Hours
A discussion of some of the factors to be considered when establishing employee work schedules

Time Reporting Procedures
A discussion of the methods for recording an employee's hours

The Uniform and Dress Code
A description of the specific dress requirements for employees

Establishing Personnel Policies
A discussion of the importance of setting personnel policies

Personnel Policy Worksheet
A worksheet of topics that assists the franchisee in developing personnel policies of his own

Evaluating Employees
A discussion detailing how to conduct employee evaluations, how often they should be done, and the records that should be kept

Discipline and Termination
Appropriate techniques to follow when disciplining and/or terminating an employee, and any forms that should accompany these actions

D. DAILY STORE PROCEDURES

Introduction

Suggested Store Hours
The recommended hours of operation for all franchises

Daily Opening and Closing Duties
The steps that are necessary to prepare for the store's daily opening and closing

The Features of the Cash Register/Point-of-Sale System
A brief description of the system and its capabilities

Procedures for Accepting Payment
How to handle various forms of payment (cash, checks, credit cards, gift certificates, travelers checks, layaways, etc.)

Merchandise Returns, Refunds, and Exchanges
An outline of the franchisor's prescribed policies in these areas

The Daily Cash Report
> The procedure for completing a cash report, along with a sample form

Preparing the Bank Deposit
> The steps to follow when preparing a deposit

Franchise Reporting Requirements and Procedures
> As required by the franchise agreement, the weekly, monthly, quarterly, and annual reports the franchisee must submit to the franchisor

Statement of Gross Receipts
> A sample of the form the franchisee completes and sends to the franchisor along with royalty payment

Advertising Activity Report
> A sample of the form the franchisee completes and sends to the franchisor with the invoices to prove that the minimum required amount (as noted in the franchise agreement) has been spent on local advertising

Preparing Financial Statements
> Introduction to general ledger reports, profit and loss statements, and balance sheets; definitions of terms and how to prepare these reports

The Chart of Accounts

The Income Statement
> A sample income statement format

The Balance Sheet
> A sample balance sheet format

Sales Practices
> A description of the sales practices

Customer Service
> A description of the prescribed methods for properly and politely dealing with customers

Product Knowledge
> A discussion on the importance of being familiar with the products of the business to properly service the customer

Handling Customer Complaints
> How to deal properly and effectively with customer complaints and concerns

Ordering and Receiving Procedures
> The procedures for ordering and receiving product

Using Approved Sources
> A discussion explaining how the franchisee is to use the sources approved by the franchisor

> List of Approved Suppliers

> Notice of Proposed Change of Supplier/Supplies

Conducting Inventory
> How to maintain an accurate accounting of the stock

> Inventory Form

Merchandising Displays
> Basic guidelines for properly displaying merchandise

Pricing the Merchandise
> Franchisor-provided guidelines for properly pricing merchandise

> Discounts
> A description of the recommended employee discount policy

Special Promotions and Sales

Cleaning and Maintenance
> Guidelines for maintaining a clean store

Safety and Security
> Guidelines for dealing with fire, theft, shoplifting, etc.

E. ADVERTISING

The Advertising Program
A discussion of the program's components, including local and national advertising

Advertising Activity Report
A form the franchisee completes and sends to the franchisor with the invoices to prove that the minimum required amount (as noted in the franchise agreement) has been spent on local advertising

The Value of Advertising
A discussion of the value and benefits that are derived from a well-planned advertising program

Guidelines for Using Marks
How to properly display the trademarks

The Grand Opening
A reiteration of the required amount of money expended on grand opening advertising as required in the franchise agreement and a discussion on how the franchisor will design a grand opening for each franchisee

Advertising Media
The media forms recommended by franchisor (yellow pages, newspapers and magazines, direct mail, radio, television, specialty advertising, publicity, etc.)

Sample Ads
Examples of franchisee ads

Obtaining Approval for Advertising Concepts and Materials
The procedures for obtaining approval for franchisee-developed advertising concepts and materials

Ordering Advertising Materials for the Corporate Office
The procedures to follow when ordering advertising materials from the franchisor

Sources of
Financing

Small Business Investment Companies
Investment Division
Small Business Administration
409 3d Street, SW, 6th floor
Washington, DC 20416
202–205–6526

National Association of Investment Companies
1111 14th Street, NW, Suite 700
Washington, DC 20005
202–289–4336

Government Programs and Loans
Small Business Administration
Office of Financial Institutions
409 3d Street, SW, Room 8033
Washington, DC 20416
202–205–6493

Minorities/Women
U.S. Department of Commerce
Minority Business Development Agency
Information Clearinghouse
14th Street and Constitution Avenue, NW, Room 6707
Washington, DC 20230
202–482–1936

Veterans
VETFRAN
Veterans Transition Franchise Initiative
Charles Wood, VETFRAN Administrator
1010 University Parks Drive
Waco, TX 76707
817–753–4555
FAX 817–756–7759

Franchisors
THE SPROUT GROUP
Patrick Boroian
140 Broadway
New York, NY 10005
212-504-3000
FAX 212-504-3444

Sources of Information

Association of Small Business Development Centers
Membership Services
Michael May, Membership Services Director
1313 Farnam, Suite 132
Omaha, NE 68182–0472
402–595–2387
FAX 402–595–2388

Bureau of Consumer Protection
Federal Trade Commission
6th Street & Pennsylvania Avenue, NW
Washington, DC 20580
202–326–2968

International Franchise Association

1350 New York Avenue, NW, Suite 900
Washington, DC 20005
202–628–8000
FAX 202–628–0812

Office of External Affairs
U.S. Small Business Administration

409 3d Street, SW, 7th floor
Washington, DC 20416
202–205–6607
FAX 202–205–7064

Appendix VI

Bibliography

Answers to the Twenty-One Most Commonly Asked Questions About Franchising (Washington: International Franchise Association, 1987).

Axelrad, Norma D. and Lewis G. Rudnick. *Franchising: A Planning and Sales Compliance Manual* (Washington: International Franchise Association, 1987).

Boroian, Donald, and Patrick Boroian. *The Franchise Advantage* (Chicago: National BestSeller Corporation, 1987).

Franchise Marketing & Sales Survey (Chicago: DePaul University and Francorp Inc., 1991).

Franchising in Europe, 1988–1990 (London: Euromonitor Publications, 1987).

Bibliography

Franchising in the Economy: 1988–1990 (Washington: International Franchise Association, 1990).

Glossary of Franchising Terms (Washington: International Franchise Association, 1988).

Investigate Before Investing (Washington: International Franchise Association, 1989).

Love, John F. *McDonald's: Behind the Arches* (New York: Bantam Books, 1986).

Luxemburg, Stan. *Roadside Empires* (New York: Penguin, 1986).

Mancuso, Joe. *How to Start, Finance, and Manage Your Own Small Business* (New York: Simon & Schuster/Prentice Hall Press, 1986).

Mancuso, Joe. *How to Write a Winning Business Plan* (New York: Simon & Schuster, 1988).

Mancuso, Joe. *Running a Family Business* (New York: Simon & Schuster, 1991).

Marshall Group Executive Search Corporation. *Franchise Executive Compensation Survey* (Washington: International Franchise Association, 1987).

McIntosh, Robert K. *Is Franchising for You?* (Washington: International Franchise Association, 1989).

Monaghan, Thomas. *Pizza Tiger* (New York: Random House, 1987).

1988–1989 Franchise Sales Executive Compensation Survey (Crete, IL: Franchise Recruiters, Ltd., 1988).

Stigelman, C. R. *Franchise Index/Profile: A Franchise Evaluation Process,* Small Business Management Series No. 35 (Washington: Small Business Administration, 1986).

Franchise Directories

Bond, Robert and Christopher. *The Source Book of Franchise Opportunities* (Homewood, IL: Dow Jones-Irwin).

Entrepreneur's Guide to Franchise & Business Opportunities (Irvine CA: Entrepreneur, Inc.).

The Franchise Annual (Lewiston, NY: INFO Press, Inc.).

The Franchise Handbook (Milwaukee: Enterprise Magazines, Inc.).

Franchise Opportunities Guide (Washington: International Franchise Association)

Suggested Periodicals

Entrepreneur (Irvine, CA: Entrepreneur, Inc.).

Franchise Update (Los Gatos, CA: Franchise Update, Inc.).

Franchising World (Washington: International Franchise Association).

INC (New York: INC. Magazine).

INFO Franchise Newsletter (New York: INFO Press, Inc.)

Success (New York: Hal Holdings, Corporation).

Appendix VII

State Franchising Regulatory Agencies

CALIFORNIA

Department of Corporations
3700 Wilshire Boulevard, 6th Floor
Los Angeles, CA 90010
213–736–2741
Index department records & copy work:
213–736–2481

Department of Corporations
1390 Market Street
San Francisco, CA 94102
415–557–8548
Index department: 415–557–3131
FAX 415–557–7166

CONNECTICUT
State of Connecticut
Department of Banking
44 Capitol Avenue
Hartford, CT 06106
203–566–4560

FLORIDA
Florida Department of Agriculture
Division of Consumer Services
Mayo Building
Tallahassee, FL 32399–0800
904–488–2221

HAWAII
Business Regulations Division
Department of Commerce and Consumer Affairs
P.O. Box 40
Honolulu, HI 96810

ILLINOIS
Attorney General's Office
500 S. Second Street
Springfield, IL 62706
217–782–4465
FAX 217–524–2987

General Information:
Secretary of State's Office
Corporate Information Division
217–782–6961

INDIANA
Chief Deputy Commissioner
Indiana Securities Division
302 W. Washington, Room E111
Indianapolis, IN 46204
317–232–6684

FAX 317–233–3675

MAINE

Bureau of Banking
Securities Division
State House Station 121
Augusta, ME 04333
207–582–8760

Business Opportunity Examiner:
207–582–8760

MARYLAND
Franchise Examiner
Office of the Attorney General
Securities Division
200 Saint Paul Place
Baltimore, Maryland 21202-2020
410–576–6360

MICHIGAN
Consumer Protection Division
Franchise Division
Department of the Attorney General
670 Law Building
525 West Ottawa Street
Lansing, MI 48913
517–373–7117

MINNESOTA
Commissioner of Commerce
Department of Commerce
Securities Division
133 East 7th Street
St. Paul, MN 55101

Commerce Analyst,
Franchise Registration
612–296–6328

Renewals
612–296–4520

NEW YORK

State of New York

Department of Law
120 Broadway, 23d Floor
New York, NY 10271
Attn: Bureau of Investor Protection and Securities
212–416–8211

For records information:
212–416–8191

NORTH CAROLINA

Office of the Secretary of State

300 North Salisbury Street, Room 302
Raleigh, NC 27065–5909
919–733–3955

NORTH DAKOTA

Securities Commissioner

State Capitol Building, 5th Floor
600 East Boulevard
Bismarck, ND 58505
701–224–4712

RHODE ISLAND

Department of Business Regulation

Division of Securities
233 Richmond Street, Suite 232
Providence, RI 02903
401–277–3048

SOUTH CAROLINA

Office of the Secretary of State

P.O. Box 11350
Columbia, SC 29211
803–734–2169

SOUTH DAKOTA
Franchise Administrator
Division of Securities
118 West Capitol
Pierre, SD 57501–2017
605–773–4823

TEXAS
Secretary of State
Business Opportunities Section
P.O. Box 12887
Austin, TX 78711
512–475–1769

Business Opportunities Section
512–463–5559

VIRGINIA
Division of Securities & Retail Franchising
P.O. Box 1197
Richmond, VA 23209
804–786–7751

WASHINGTON
Department of Licensing Securities Division
P.O. Box 9033
Olympia, WA 98507–9033
206–753–6928

WISCONSIN
Office of the Commissioner of Securities
101 East Wilson Street, 4th floor
Box 1768
Madison, WI 53702
698–266–3364

ALBERTA, CANADA
Alberta Securities Commission
10025 Jasper Avenue, 21st floor

Edmonton, Alberta
Canada T5J 3Z5
403–427–5201
FAX 403–422–0777

Index

Index

About the Authors

Joseph R. Mancuso is the founder of the not-for-profit Center for Entrepreneurial Management, Inc. (CEM) and the Chief Executive Officers Club (CEO Club). He has also founded seven businesses, is a member of the board of advisors for forty U.S. companies, and often speaks to groups about entrepreneurship.

He holds an Electrical Engineering degree from Worcester Polytechnic Institute, an MBA from the Harvard Business School, and has a doctorate in Educational Administration from Boston University. He has edited or authored more than twenty-one books, including *How to Start, Finance, and Manage Your Own Small Business, How to Write a Winning Business Plan,* and *How to Get a Business Loan (Without Signing Your Life Away).* He lives in Manhattan with his wife and business partner, Karla, and their children Max and May.

Donald D. Boroian is Chairman and Chief Executive Officer of Francorp, Inc., a Chicago-based international consultancy that has provided services for more than 4,500 businesses, including some of the nation's best-known franchisors: ARCO's am/pm mini markets, Hershey Foods, Omni Hotels, Texaco, and Valvoline. Additionally, his companies have provided full franchise development programs for more than 500 businesses. With more than thirty years of experience in corporate management, franchising, direct sales, and business administration, he is among the nation's most sought-after consultants in the field of business expansion. He gives frequent seminars on franchising and expansion strategies to colleges, universities, and trade groups.

He is a graduate of DePaul University, and continued his postgraduate studies at DePaul and the University of Chicago Executive MBA program. His first book, *The Franchise Advantage,* is widely regarded as one of the most authoritative books on franchise development.